11+ English

For Ages 10-11
Practice Paper 5

For GL Assessment

Read the following:

Do not open this booklet or start the test until you are told to do so.

1. This is a multiple-choice test.

2. There are 50 questions and you will have 50 minutes to do the test.

3. You should mark your answer to each question in pencil on the separate answer sheet.

4. You should only mark one answer for each question. To mark your answer, draw a straight line through the rectangle next to the option you have chosen. If you make a mistake, rub it out and mark your new answer clearly.

5. Make sure you keep your place on the answer sheet and mark your answer in the box that has the same number as the question.

6. Do as many questions as you can. If you get stuck on a question, choose the answer that you think is most likely to be correct, then move on to the next question.

7. You should do any rough working on a separate piece of paper.

Work carefully, but go as quickly as you can.

Read this passage carefully and answer the questions that follow.

The *Castellers* of Catalonia

Across Catalonia, a region in the north-east of Spain, a remarkable display takes place at cultural festivals. In town squares and arenas, people work together
5 to form structures that resemble giant human pyramids. These magnificent, vibrant towers called *castells* (the Catalan word for 'castles') are an impressive sight, reaching high into the air.

10 The people who participate in the *castell*-building tradition are called *castellers*. They work in teams to form towers that can be nine or even ten levels high, with the sturdiest and heaviest
15 people at the base and smaller, lighter people higher up. The teams climb to the accompaniment of traditional Catalan music, played on flutes and drums, with the melody changing as each level is built.
20 A child clambers to the apex of each tower and raises their hand in a salute when the construction is complete. Deconstructing the towers is equally important and is often a more perilous part of the spectacle
25 — it takes plenty of concentration and practice.

The *castellers* wear a uniform composed of white trousers, a red bandana and a coloured shirt to identify
30 which team they belong to. The most important part of their outfit is a black sash wrapped around the waist. This serves a dual function, providing the wearer with back support and offering other team
35 members a foothold as they climb up the tower.

The *castellers*' skill and daring are vital to the success of their towers, but these astonishing structures are also
40 held together by a powerful team spirit.

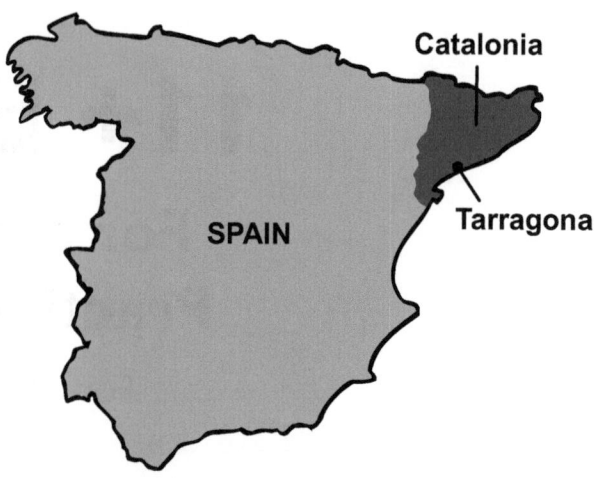

Although *castellers* come from a wide variety of backgrounds, they all embrace the tradition's core values of strength, balance, courage and wisdom. Thanks to
45 these shared values, the *castell* tradition helps to foster a sense of solidarity and community spirit in the towns and cities where it takes place.

For Catalonia's most ambitious teams,
50 *castell*-building goes beyond culture and community — it is also a highly competitive sport. Every two years, a tournament takes place in the Catalan city of Tarragona to see which team can
55 build the best tower. Judges award marks to each team based on the height and difficulty of their tower, as well as their construction technique. After several rounds, the best teams compete in the
60 final to claim that year's title. For the thousands of spectators who crowd the stadium to watch the tournament, it is a thrilling, heart-stopping display of skill, strength and courage.

Answer these questions about the text. You can refer back to the text if you need to.
Pick the best answer and mark its letter on your answer sheet.

1 The *castells* are described as "magnificent, vibrant towers" (lines 6-7). This suggests that:

    A   they are luxurious and energetic.
    B   they are impressive and colourful.
    C   they are precarious and bright.
    D   they are tall and unsteady.
    E   they are rich and sparkling.

2 According to the text, what is often the most dangerous part of a *castell*-building display?

    A   Constructing the base
    B   Adding more levels to the tower
    C   Including children in the tower
    D   Building the tower in time to music
    E   Dismantling the tower

3 What is the purpose of the sash that the *castellers* wear?

    A   It reflects their team identity.
    B   It offers spinal support.
    C   It represents their shared values.
    D   It makes a political statement.
    E   It makes climbing the tower more challenging.

4 According to the text, which of the following is not a core value of the tradition?

    A   Strength
    B   Wisdom
    C   Solidarity
    D   Balance
    E   Courage

5 In the *castell*-building tournament, which two of the following are the teams judged on?

    1) Their popularity with the crowd
    2) The height of their tower
    3) The method used to build their tower
    4) How many people are used in their tower
    5) How competitive they are

    A   1 and 2
    B   1 and 5
    C   2 and 3
    D   2 and 4
    E   3 and 5

Turn over to the next page

6 The *castell*-building tournament is described as a "heart-stopping display" (line 63). This means that:

    A   the tournament involves vigorous exercise.
    B   the tournament is bad for people's health.
    C   the tournament is thrilling to watch.
    D   the tournament is exhausting.
    E   the tournament is comforting.

7 Which of the following is not mentioned in the text?

    A   *Castell* means 'castle' in English.
    B   *Castells* can have at least eight levels.
    C   Music is played while the *castells* are built.
    D   A single *castell* can involve hundreds of people.
    E   The *castell*-building tournament happens every other year.

8 Where would you be most likely to find this text?

    A   In a dictionary
    B   In a history textbook
    C   In a travel guide
    D   In a fashion magazine
    E   In a Spanish cookbook

Answer these questions about the meaning of words as they are used in the text.

9 What does the word "apex" (line 20) mean?

    A   The highest point
    B   The widest point
    C   The middle
    D   The lowest point
    E   The narrowest point

10 Which of these words is closest in meaning to "foster" (line 46)?

    A   Banish
    B   Encourage
    C   Lift
    D   Advertise
    E   Exaggerate

Answer these questions about the way words and phrases are used in the text.

11 "Across Catalonia, a region in the north-east of Spain, a remarkable display takes place at cultural festivals" (lines 1-3). Which of the following is the subject of the sentence?

    A Catalonia
    B a region
    C the north-east of Spain
    D a remarkable display
    E cultural festivals

12 What type of words are these?

concentration   success   culture   difficulty

    A Abstract nouns
    B Idioms
    C Verbs
    D Adjectives
    E Synonyms

13 "For the thousands of spectators who crowd the stadium to watch the tournament, it is a thrilling, heart-stopping display of skill, strength and courage" (lines 60-64). What type of word is "crowd" in this sentence?

    A Adjective
    B Conjunction
    C Noun
    D Verb
    E Adverb

Turn over to the next page

Read this passage carefully and answer the questions that follow.

An Unusual Haunting

"Do we really have to go in there?"
Imran asked sheepishly. His older sister
Aaliyah sighed in annoyance. She was
determined to put a stop to his ridiculous
5   notions about the supposed ghostly
goings-on in the old library.

"All these rumours are complete
nonsense," she insisted. "There's
nothing lurking in there but a bunch of
10 unwanted, dusty books and I'm going to
prove it." She guided her brother along
the deserted, dingy corridor that snaked
towards the library, the final resting place
for long-forgotten school books.

15 When the door finally loomed out of
the shadows, Imran started to drag his
feet. His friends took great delight in filling
his head with terrifying tales about this
place, and the last thing he wanted was to
20 experience it first hand. Heedless of his
feelings, Aaliyah grasped the door handle
and confidently swung the door open.

The room had several sash windows
which were obscured by metres of
25 moth-eaten curtain. Only a few slivers
of light were able to penetrate the
gloom, but it was just enough to make
out the shelves, clutching their burden
of abandoned books. Aaliyah ran her
30 fingers cautiously over the wall and
found a light switch. She flicked it on,
but nothing happened. Imran groaned
and shuffled over to the nearest window.
Beyond the school fence, he could see
35 the brown, withered grass of a dilapidated
graveyard, with row upon row of crumbling
headstones. What a fitting view, he
thought, for such a decidedly creepy room.

On the other side of the library, Aaliyah
40 was tiptoeing down one of the aisles,
scanning every nook and cranny. As
she reached the final shelf, she became
aware of a strange, uneven tapping sound
behind her. It was very muffled to begin
45 with, but it slowly became louder and
more insistent.

"That's not funny, Imran," she hissed,
turning around. To her surprise, her
brother was still by the window, his hands
50 clutching his rucksack. The tapping
started again and Aaliyah frowned as
she tried desperately to pinpoint its
location. She had just taken a few
tentative steps towards it when there
55 was an almighty crash and a stack of
paperbacks cascaded onto the floor.

She shrieked and bolted for the door.
Imran stood frozen to the spot, his worst
fears suddenly coming to life. Just as
60 Aaliyah grabbed his arm, a cheerful
"meow" echoed from the back of the
room. The siblings whirled around and
watched, astonished, as the caretaker's
sprightly tabby cat trotted towards them.

Answer these questions about the text. You can refer back to the text if you need to.
Pick the best answer and mark its letter on your answer sheet.

14 At the start of the text, how does Aaliyah feel about the ghostly activity in the old library?

    A   She finds it frightening.
    B   She is annoyed that it happens.
    C   She thinks that it doesn't really happen.
    D   She wants to put a stop to it.
    E   She wants to prove that it really happens.

15 When Imran sees the library door, he starts "to drag his feet" (lines 16-17).
This suggests that:

    A   he is feeling apprehensive.
    B   he is feeling tired.
    C   he is feeling relaxed.
    D   he is annoyed with his sister.
    E   he is in pain.

16 Imran's friends "took great delight" (line 17) in telling him "terrifying tales" (line 18) about the old library. This suggests that:

    A   they wanted Imran to investigate the old library.
    B   they thought Imran was interested in the old library.
    C   they wanted to reassure Imran about the old library.
    D   they liked to tease Imran about the old library.
    E   they liked talking about the old library.

17 Which two of the following tell you that it is dark inside the old library?

    1) It is at the end of a dingy corridor.
    2) There are curtains covering the windows.
    3) The door to it is in the shadows.
    4) The shelves are piled high with books.
    5) The light isn't working.

    A   1 and 2
    B   1 and 3
    C   2 and 5
    D   3 and 4
    E   3 and 5

18 Why is the graveyard described as "a fitting view" (line 37) for the old library?

    A   It looks like a nicer place than the old library.
    B   It is another place that Imran doesn't want to visit.
    C   It can be seen clearly from the old library.
    D   It is also full of dusty objects.
    E   It looks just as spooky as the old library.

Turn over to the next page

19 How does the tapping sound change?

    A   It is behind Aaliyah at first and gradually moves in front of her.
    B   It is slow at first and gradually gets faster.
    C   It is uneven at first and slowly becomes more regular.
    D   It is quiet at first and gradually gets louder.
    E   It is very muffled at first and then it suddenly stops.

20 Which adverb best describes how Aaliyah moves towards the tapping sound?

    A   Desperately
    B   Hesitantly
    C   Confidently
    D   Eagerly
    E   Angrily

21 After the books fell onto the floor, Aaliyah "bolted for the door" (line 57).
This tells us that:

    A   she wanted to lock the door.
    B   she wanted to leave the room immediately.
    C   she wanted to check the door for clues.
    D   she wanted to stop Imran from leaving her alone.
    E   she wanted to make sure the door wasn't locked.

Answer these questions about the way words and phrases are used in the text.

22 The library shelves are described as "clutching their burden
of abandoned books" (lines 28-29). This is an example of:

    A   onomatopoeia.
    B   exaggeration.
    C   an idiom.
    D   a simile.
    E   personification.

23 What type of words are these?

complete   **dingy**   **withered**   **almighty**

    A   Nouns
    B   Adverbs
    C   Adjectives
    D   Verbs
    E   Pronouns

Answer these questions about the meaning of words as they are used in the text.

24 Which of these words is closest in meaning to "dilapidated" (line 35)?

 A Ancient
 B Antique
 C Overgrown
 D Run-down
 E Abandoned

25 The word "cascaded" (line 56) could most accurately be replaced by:

 A tumbled.
 B settled.
 C scrambled.
 D rolled.
 E trickled.

26 Which of these words is closest in meaning to "sprightly" (line 64)?

 A Friendly
 B Elderly
 C Energetic
 D Mischievous
 E Curious

Turn over to the next page

This passage contains some spelling mistakes. Each numbered line has either one mistake or no mistake. For each line, work out which group of words contains a mistake and mark the letter on your answer sheet. Mark N if there is no mistake.

Superb Socks

Dear Uncle Haruki,

27 I am writing to express my gratitude for the extrordinary socks you recently sent for
    A   B   C   D   N

28 my birthday. It is no exageration to say that they are unquestionably the most fabulous
    A   B   C   D   N

29 gift I have ever recieved. As well as being stylish and exceptionally comfortable,
    A   B   C   D   N

30 they are also warm enough to ensure that my feet remain cosy in even the bitterest
    A   B   C   D   N

31 whether — an essential feature in these Arctic conditions. As you can imagine,
    A   B   C   D   N

32 my fellow explorers were incredibly envious when they saw me sporting my new
    A   B   C   D   N

33 footwear, and several of them have tried to perswade me to part with my splendid socks.
    A   B   C   D   N

34 Few people appreciate a top-quality sock as much as a profesional polar adventurer.
    A   B   C   D   N

Thank you again for your very thoughtful gift,

With love and best wishes,

Emelia

This passage contains some mistakes involving capital letters and punctuation.
Each numbered line has either one mistake or no mistake. For each line, work out
which group of words contains a mistake and mark the letter on your answer sheet.
Mark N if there is no mistake.

Stuck in the Mud

35 "Wait!" wailed Tim forlornly "I'm stuck! I can't move my foot — it just keeps sinking!"
  A   B   C   D   N

36 Mum sighed. Their walking holiday wasnt going well. Instead of the sunshine and glorious
          A   B   C   D   N

37 views she had imagined, they had encountered nothing but rain, cows and, endless mud.
          A   B   C   D   N

38 Scowling, she stomped over to Tim, whose left foot was submerged in the sludge
          A   B   C   D   N

39 "You can't be stuck" she insisted, taking hold of his leg and giving it a firm tug. It didn't
          A   B   C   D   N

40 move. She tugged again, harder this time. Still nothing. Adjusting her grip she pulled at
          A   B   C   D   N

41 his leg with all her might. With a loud squelching sound, Tims' foot emerged and they both
          A   B   C   D   N

42 flew backwards, landing in yet another deep puddle of thick, sticky, clinging, brown muck.
          A   B   C   D   N

"See, I told you that you weren't stuck," Mum muttered, wiping the dirt from her face.

Turn over to the next page

For each numbered line, choose the word, or group of words, which completes the passage correctly. The passage needs to make sense and be written in correct English. Pick one of the five options and mark the letter on your answer sheet.

Kaninhoppning

43 Rabbit agility has its **originated** **origins** **origined** **original** **originate** in Sweden,
        A   **B**   **C**   **D**   **E**

44 where it is known as Kaninhoppning. **The** **That** **Those** **Them** **Their** sport is modelled
        A   **B**   **C**   **D**   **E**

45 on horse show jumping. Rabbits are **teaching** **teacher** **teaches** **taught** **teach**
        A   **B**   **C**   **D**   **E**

46 to negotiate a series of obstacles **with** **without** **within** **while** **when** a set time.
        A   **B**   **C**   **D**   **E**

47 The obstacles can be up to half a metre high, **although** **whereas** **whether** **if** **despite**
        A   **B**   **C**   **D**   **E**

48 some rabbits can jump much **high** **highs** **highest** **highly** **higher** than this.
        A   **B**   **C**   **D**   **E**

49 The sport **has spread** **is spreading** **spreads** **was spread** **spreaded** widely
        A   **B**   **C**   **D**   **E**

50 since its **emerges** **emergance** **emergence** **emerged** **emerge** in the 1970s,
        A   **B**   **C**   **D**   **E**

and there are now rabbit agility organisations all over the world.

End of Test

11+ English

For Ages 10-11
Practice Paper 6

For GL Assessment

Read the following:

Do not open this booklet or start the test until you are told to do so.

1. This is a multiple-choice test.

2. There are 50 questions and you will have 50 minutes to do the test.

3. You should mark your answer to each question in pencil on the separate answer sheet.

4. You should only mark one answer for each question. To mark your answer,
    draw a straight line through the rectangle next to the option you have chosen.
    If you make a mistake, rub it out and mark your new answer clearly.

5. Make sure you keep your place on the answer sheet and mark your
    answer in the box that has the same number as the question.

6. Do as many questions as you can. If you get stuck on a question, choose the answer
    that you think is most likely to be correct, then move on to the next question.

7. You should do any rough working on a separate piece of paper.

Work carefully, but go as quickly as you can.

Read this passage carefully and answer the questions that follow.

The Rise of Palm Oil

What is palm oil?

Palm oil is a type of vegetable oil that's extracted from the fruit of the oil palm tree, a tropical plant native to Africa. It's been
5 used for thousands of years as a cooking oil, but more recently it's become a key ingredient in everyday products including margarine, ice cream, fast food, packaged snacks and even cleaning products. So
10 it's no surprise that palm oil now accounts for 40% of vegetable oil consumption worldwide, and with palm-oil-rich products becoming more popular in countries all over the world, there is an ever-increasing
15 demand for it.

A replacement ingredient

Palm oil is a very versatile product, and this has allowed it to become a standard addition to a huge number
20 of goods available on supermarket shelves. Some of its numerous practical uses include giving food a longer shelf life, stopping ice cream from melting too quickly and making shampoo foam.
25 However, it hasn't always been a go-to ingredient. Traditionally, companies used animal by-products such as tallow (animal fat) instead. Tallow is packed with essential vitamins and
30 fatty acids which are good for the skin — this makes it ideal for soaps, body creams and other beauty products. It also has many different culinary uses, from deep frying to pastry making.
35 However, a growing trend for more plant-based ingredients triggered a move away from tallow and opened the door to palm oil. Companies saw it as an attractive alternative because

40 it could be used in exactly the same way as tallow, it was less expensive to buy and it was initially thought to be better for the environment.

The benefits of palm oil

45 Palm oil production is very efficient when compared to other vegetable oils. The amount of land needed to produce high quantities of oil is much smaller than you might expect. For example,
50 one football pitch of oil palm trees can produce just over three tonnes of palm oil. In order to produce the same amount of coconut oil, you'd need almost five times as much land.
55 With the world's population predicted to expand to 9.7 billion people by 2050, farmers need to produce more food from their land. Choosing efficient crops like palm oil is one way to make sure that
60 there will be enough food for everyone in the future. Moreover, because oil palm trees use less land than other oil-producing crops, growing them can help to limit the impact that vegetable
65 oil production has on the environment.
In poorer countries, palm oil is helping to generate money for local communities.

Oil palm plantations provide farmers with a steady and secure source of income, and many of them rely on the industry to provide for their families.

A controversial crop

On the other hand, palm oil does have its disadvantages. Despite the efficiency of palm oil production, it can still have a major impact on the environment. In Indonesia and Malaysia, which produce around 85% of the world's palm oil, millions of trees have been cleared to make way for oil palm plantations. This deforestation releases lots of greenhouse gases (like carbon dioxide) into the atmosphere. Extra greenhouse gases can contribute to global warming by trapping too much heat in the atmosphere.

Furthermore, deforestation for palm oil plantations is adding to the threats faced by some of Southeast Asia's most iconic animals. The Sumatran tiger and the Bornean orangutan, for example, are already in danger due to hunting and habitat loss from logging, and palm oil is putting extra pressure on the dwindling forests that these animals call home.

It's not just animals that are affected by this booming industry — many indigenous communities who live in and rely on the rainforests for survival are being forced out of their homes to make way for oil palm plantations.

Palm oil in a sustainable future

Now that palm oil has become such an integral part of modern life, it's unlikely that we'll stop using it in the future. It's estimated that global palm oil production will increase by more than 300% in the next three decades, and producers are already expanding into new areas to try to keep up with demand. To ensure that this growth isn't to the detriment of the environment, organisations like the Roundtable on Sustainable Palm Oil (RSPO) are working to promote sustainable production of palm oil without deforestation. So far, nearly 20% of global palm oil is RSPO certified.

In addition to preventing deforestation, other initiatives have been introduced to protect endangered species that have been affected by palm oil production. For example, in Malaysia, efforts are underway to replant unused land with native forest species to create wildlife corridors, which will connect isolated patches of forest together. This will help to protect Malaysia's elephants, which need large areas of land for foraging, by giving them safe pathways between different areas of forest. It will also prevent conflict between elephants and humans by keeping the elephants away from oil palm plantations, where they can cause significant damage to the valuable oil palm trees.

However, there is still more work to be done. While many companies worldwide are making a clear move towards sustainably sourced palm oil, others seem reluctant to change. In part, this is because sustainable palm oil costs more to produce, which in turn makes it more expensive to buy. If a company has to spend more money acquiring palm oil, their end product, be it food or cosmetics, will also have a higher price tag, and many companies are uncertain whether customers would be willing to pay more for their favourite products.

Turn over to the next page

Answer these questions about the text. You can refer back to the text if you need to.
Pick the best answer and mark its letter on your answer sheet.

1   Where does palm oil come from?

    A   The leaves of the oil palm tree
    B   The fruit of the oil palm tree
    C   A plant that only grows in cold places
    D   Vegetable oils
    E   Oils used for cooking

2   Which of these products containing palm oil is not mentioned in the text?

    A   Fast food
    B   Cleaning products
    C   Packaged snacks
    D   Margarine
    E   Chocolate

3   Which of these statements is true?

    A   People have only recently started using palm oil.
    B   Most countries are using less palm oil than they used to.
    C   Just under half of all the vegetable oil used worldwide is palm oil.
    D   Oil palm trees are native to Australia.
    E   Palm oil has been a key ingredient in many everyday products for thousands of years.

4   Which two of the following are given as examples of the benefits of palm oil?

    1) It allows shops to buy more food.
    2) It makes food last longer before it goes bad.
    3) It makes shampoo less runny.
    4) It makes ice cream melt more slowly.
    5) It makes ice cream taste better.

    A   1 and 2
    B   1 and 4
    C   2 and 3
    D   2 and 4
    E   3 and 5

5   According to the text, tallow:

    A   is not a versatile product.
    B   is harmful to the skin.
    C   cannot be consumed by people.
    D   comes from animals.
    E   is only used in beauty products.

6 According to the text, what caused companies to stop using tallow?

A Their customers thought tallow was too expensive.
B Their customers preferred the taste of palm oil.
C Their customers thought palm oil was better for the environment.
D Many of their customers became vegetarian.
E Their customers wanted more plant-based ingredients in their products.

7 According to the text, which of the following is a benefit of palm oil?

A Palm oil production uses five times as much land as coconut oil production.
B One oil palm tree can produce just over three tonnes of palm oil.
C Oil palm trees are smaller than you might expect.
D Palm oil production uses less land than other vegetable oils.
E Palm oil production doesn't affect the environment.

8 Which of the following is given as a reason why we will need to grow more efficient crops in the future?

A Growing crops will become more expensive.
B There will be more people to feed.
C Efficient crops are easier to grow.
D It will take longer to grow food.
E Efficient crops give farmers a reliable income.

9 Why is palm oil described as "A controversial crop" (line 72)?

A Because it is used in a huge number of products.
B Because it has replaced tallow in many products.
C Because it is produced in lots of different countries.
D Because most global palm oil is not RSPO certified.
E Because there are drawbacks to producing it.

10 According to the text, Indonesia and Malaysia:

A produce more palm oil than anywhere else.
B have the fewest palm oil plantations.
C have cleared millions of oil palm trees.
D do not produce any greenhouse gases.
E produce all of the world's palm oil.

Turn over to the next page

11 Deforestation causes:

A the atmosphere to create more greenhouse gases.
B lower levels of carbon dioxide in the atmosphere.
C trees to absorb more carbon dioxide.
D the atmosphere to destroy greenhouse gases.
E higher levels of greenhouse gases in the atmosphere.

12 Which of these statements is false?

A Orangutans and tigers are hunted by people.
B Palm oil production is the main threat to orangutans and tigers.
C The forests where orangutans and tigers live are disappearing.
D Palm oil production has made some indigenous communities homeless.
E Orangutans and tigers are losing their habitat because of logging.

13 It's predicted that palm oil production will:

A only increase in areas where it's already being produced.
B increase over the next thirty years.
C decrease because future demand for palm oil will drop.
D never be able to keep up with demand.
E remain unchanged in the future.

14 What is meant by the phrase "to the detriment of the environment" (lines 110-111)?

A Improving the quality of the environment
B Benefiting the environment
C Ignoring the environment
D Causing harm to the environment
E Overusing the environment

15 According to the text, what does the Roundtable on Sustainable Palm Oil (RSPO) do?

A It attempts to reduce palm oil production.
B It creates wildlife corridors.
C It encourages the production of palm oil without clearing land.
D It helps palm oil producers expand into new areas.
E It encourages people to stop using palm oil.

16 Which of the following best describes the role of a wildlife corridor?

A To allow animals to move freely between different patches of forest
B To stop humans chopping down too many trees
C To allow animals to travel between oil palm plantations
D To stop humans coming into contact with animals
E To stop animals from leaving the rainforest

17 According to the passage, some companies don't use sustainable palm oil because:

A it is difficult to find.
B it makes the end product less expensive.
C customers refuse to spend more money on the things they buy.
D it is more expensive to produce.
E customers are reluctant to buy products made with it.

18 Which of the following is not mentioned in the text?

A Where oil palm trees come from
B The products that originally used tallow
C How palm oil production is predicted to change in the future
D The percentage of global palm oil that is RSPO certified
E How to tell if palm oil is from a sustainable source

Turn over to the next page

7

Answer these questions about the meaning of words as they are used in the text.

19 Which of these words is closest in meaning to "generate" (line 67)?

    A Receive

    B Increase

    C Produce

    D Expand

    E Spend

20 Which of these words is closest in meaning to "dwindling" (line 93)?

    A Minute

    B Shrinking

    C Dispersing

    D Limiting

    E Sparse

21 Palm oil production is described as a "booming industry" (line 96). This means that:

    A it is declining.

    B it makes a lot of noise.

    C it is very large.

    D it is very successful.

    E it has advantages and disadvantages.

22 The word "reluctant" (line 139) could most accurately be replaced by:

    A unable.

    B difficult.

    C careless.

    D eager.

    E unwilling.

Answer these questions about the way words and phrases are used in the text.

23 Palm oil has "become a standard addition to a huge number of goods available on supermarket shelves" (lines 18-21). What type of word is "standard" in this sentence?

A Adjective
B Noun
C Adverb
D Determiner
E Pronoun

24 What type of words are these?

worldwide   exactly   initially   almost

A Conjunctions
B Verbs
C Adjectives
D Adverbs
E Nouns

25 "This will help to protect Malaysia's elephants, which need large areas of land for foraging" (lines 125-127). What type of word is "which" in this sentence?

A Relative pronoun
B Noun
C Preposition
D Verb
E Adverb

26 "However, there is still more work to be done" (lines 135-136).
Which word in this sentence is a determiner?

A done
B more
C there
D still
E work

Turn over to the next page

This passage contains some spelling mistakes. Each numbered line has either one mistake or no mistake. For each line, work out which group of words contains a mistake and mark the letter on your answer sheet. Mark N if there is no mistake.

A Worried Wizard

27 Wes rumaged desperately through his cupboards. What was he going to wear? His
     A   B   C   D   N

28 prefered robes — the purple ones with mystical gold symbols — had partially vanished
     A   B   C   D   N

29 after an unfortunate insident with an invisibility potion, and his second-best outfit had never
     A   B   C   D   N

30 been quite the same since that shrinking spell backfired. He didn't even have a suitable
     A   B   C   D   N

31 pointy hat. Blaze, his disobediant pet dragon, had incinerated his entire collection of
     A   B   C   D   N

32 headgear last week. At this rate, he'd be atending the Sorcerers' Ball, the most
     A   B   C   D   N

33 prestigious event in the conjuring calender, in his pyjamas. There was only one thing
     A   B   C   D   N

34 for it. Wes raced downstairs and siezed his spell book. What could possibly go wrong?
     A   B   C   D   N

This passage contains some mistakes involving capital letters and punctuation.
Each numbered line has either one mistake or no mistake. For each line, work out
which group of words contains a mistake and mark the letter on your answer sheet.
Mark N if there is no mistake.

The Grand Opening

35 Visitors will flock to Burgus on tuesday as Fortis Castle opens its doors to the public for

       A   B   C   D   N

36 the very first time. The historic castle, which was built more than 1000 years ago has long

       A   B   C   D   N

37 been in a state of disrepair. However, since it was acquired by it's current owner (Donna

       A   B   C   D   N

38 John, it has been transformed into a spectacular and fun-filled tourist attraction.

       A   B   C   D   N

39 "We can't wait to welcome visitors to the castle!" Said Ms John. "We've created so many

       A   B   C   D   N

40 exciting things for them to see and do, in the tallest turret, there's a fantastic helter-skelter;

       A   B   C   D   N

41 the gardens boast a precise replica of the castle, constructed entirely from cheese and

       A   B   C   D   N

42 you can even swim with dolphins in the moat. We really do have something for everyone.

       A   B   C   D   N

Turn over to the next page

For each numbered line, choose the word, or group of words, which completes the passage correctly. The passage needs to make sense and be written in correct English. Pick one of the five options and mark the letter on your answer sheet.

Sun, Sea and Sand

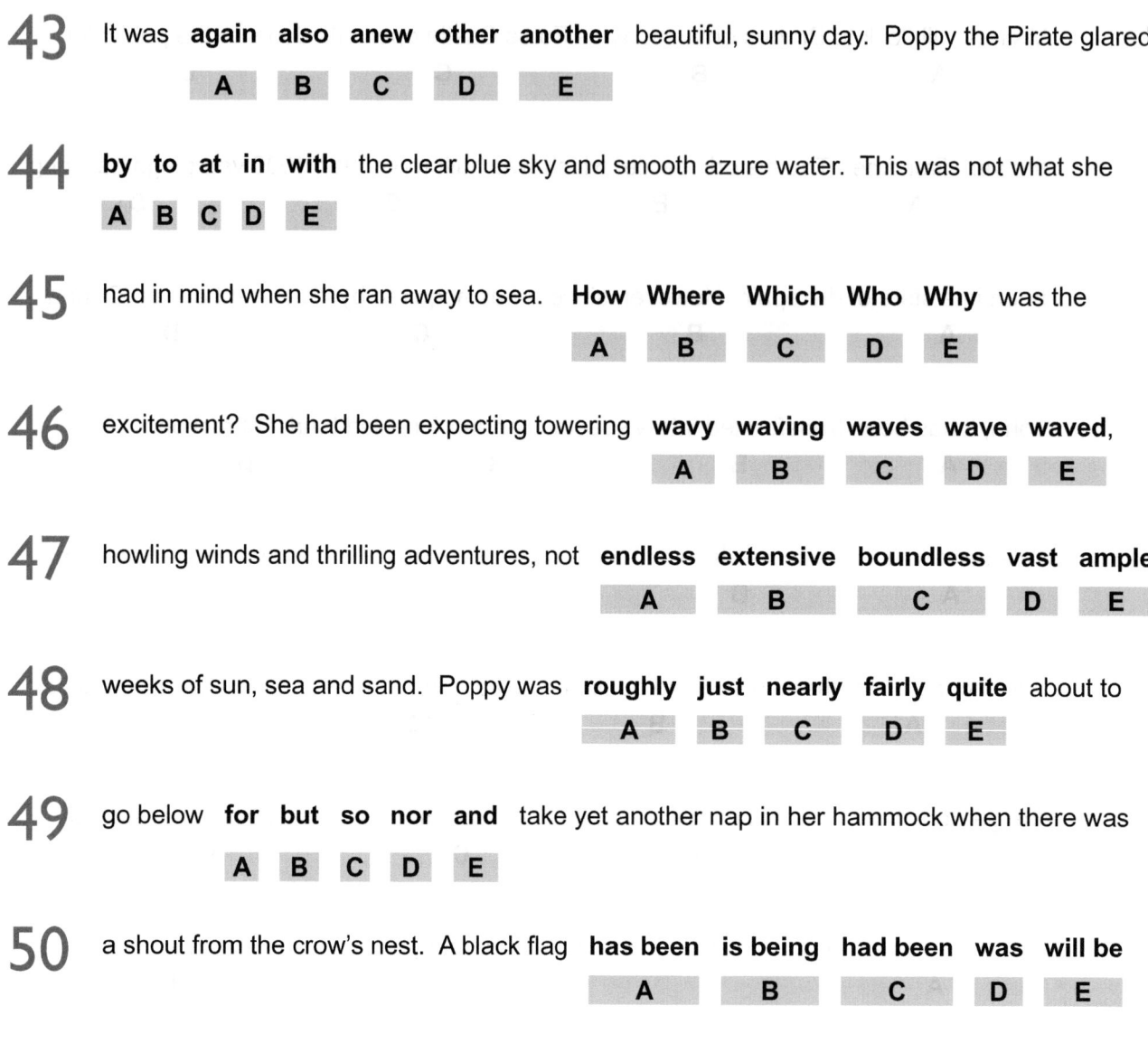

43 It was **again also anew other another** beautiful, sunny day. Poppy the Pirate glared
   A   B   C   D   E

44 **by to at in with** the clear blue sky and smooth azure water. This was not what she
   A B C D E

45 had in mind when she ran away to sea. **How Where Which Who Why** was the
   A   B   C   D   E

46 excitement? She had been expecting towering **wavy waving waves wave waved**,
   A   B   C   D   E

47 howling winds and thrilling adventures, not **endless extensive boundless vast ample**
   A   B   C   D   E

48 weeks of sun, sea and sand. Poppy was **roughly just nearly fairly quite** about to
   A   B   C   D   E

49 go below **for but so nor and** take yet another nap in her hammock when there was
   A   B   C   D   E

50 a shout from the crow's nest. A black flag **has been is being had been was will be**
   A   B   C   D   E

spotted on the horizon.

End of Test

11+ English

For Ages 10-11
Practice Paper 7

For GL Assessment

Read the following:

Do not open this booklet or start the test until you are told to do so.

1. This is a multiple-choice test.

2. There are 50 questions and you will have 50 minutes to do the test.

3. You should mark your answer to each question in pencil on the separate answer sheet.

4. You should only mark one answer for each question. To mark your answer,
   draw a straight line through the rectangle next to the option you have chosen.
   If you make a mistake, rub it out and mark your new answer clearly.

5. Make sure you keep your place on the answer sheet and mark your
   answer in the box that has the same number as the question.

6. Do as many questions as you can. If you get stuck on a question, choose the answer
   that you think is most likely to be correct, then move on to the next question.

7. You should do any rough working on a separate piece of paper.

Work carefully, but go as quickly as you can.

Read this passage carefully and answer the questions that follow.

Walsall Wolf Girl

You wouldn't be reading this if it wasn't for Mr Boateng. I only wrote the essay in the first place as a homework assignment — I never thought it would interest people.
5 He was so excited after he marked it though.

"Saffie," he insisted, "your story is going to be *monumental*!" His enthusiasm was infectious, and when he suggested that
10 I send the essay to a magazine, it was difficult to resist the idea. I didn't really think it would change anything, but then neither does howling at the moon, and I still do that from time to time.

15 I'm a werewolf, you see. Everybody thinks that werewolves are fairytale creatures, like unicorns or dragons, which is just ridiculous really. Still, it's far from the most ludicrous idea that people have
20 about werewolves. You might have heard some of them — that we can be killed by silver, or that a werewolf bite can turn you into a werewolf yourself, as if it were some kind of exotic contagious disease. They're
25 all rubbish. Just about the only thing that the stories get right is that we transform during a full moon.

All these false expectations mean that I'm a constant source of disappointment
30 to journalists. An interviewer once asked me in earnest tones whether I really eat humans when I'm in wolf form. I could only laugh at the look of dismay on his face when I told him I'm a vegetarian, just
35 like every other werewolf out there.

The media attention is something I definitely wasn't expecting when the magazine published my essay. I thought a handful of people might read it at most,

40 but for some reason it really struck a chord. The press picked up my story and before I knew it, interviews and TV appearances were crammed into my diary like sardines in a tin. The constant
45 whirlwind of media appearances is certainly exhilarating, but it can also be pretty exhausting at times. I shouldn't complain though, since it looks like all this attention is sparking some real change for
50 werewolves.

I've had countless messages from fellow werewolves telling me how glad they are that someone's finally setting the record straight. Quite a few
55 non-werewolves have also been in touch to offer their support, and a surprising number of them say that they can relate to my story. In fact, so many of them have also felt excluded or misunderstood at one
60 time or another that I've started to wonder whether humans and werewolves are actually so different after all.

Answer these questions about the text. You can refer back to the text if you need to. Pick the best answer and mark its letter on your answer sheet.

1 Why did Saffie write the essay?

    A   She wrote it because she thought it would interest people.
    B   She wrote it because she knew Mr Boateng would like it.
    C   She wrote it to get it published in a magazine.
    D   She wrote it because she thought it would change things for werewolves.
    E   She wrote it for her homework.

2 Mr Boateng said "your story is going to be *monumental*" (lines 7-8). What did he mean by this?

    A   Saffie's story was definitely going to be published.
    B   Saffie's story was going to be important.
    C   Saffie's story was going to be inconsequential.
    D   Saffie's story was going to make people laugh.
    E   Saffie's story was going to be popular.

3 According to the text, which statement about werewolves is true?

    A   Werewolves don't really exist.
    B   Werewolves can be killed by silver.
    C   Werewolves transform during a full moon.
    D   Being bitten by a werewolf turns you into a werewolf.
    E   Werewolves eat people.

4 According to the text, why does Saffie disappoint journalists?

    A   She doesn't conform to the stereotypes.
    B   She gets annoyed with them.
    C   She is bad at giving interviews.
    D   She doesn't have time for many interviews.
    E   She laughs at them.

5 Saffie's essay "really struck a chord" (lines 40-41) with people. This means that:

    A   people were outraged by it.
    B   people found it surprising.
    C   it changed people's attitudes.
    D   it caused a scandal.
    E   it made people feel sympathy for Saffie.

Turn over to the next page

6 According to the text, Saffie finds the media attention:

    A surprising and annoying.
    B draining and tedious.
    C funny and thrilling.
    D boring and irritating.
    E tiring and exciting.

7 Which adjective best describes how Saffie feels about the future for werewolves?

    A Ecstatic
    B Dejected
    C Optimistic
    D Frustrated
    E Fearful

8 What is the main thing that surprises Saffie about the messages she receives from non-werewolves?

    A She is surprised that the messages are supportive.
    B She is surprised that non-werewolves can relate to her experiences.
    C She is surprised that so many non-werewolves have been in touch with her.
    D She is surprised that non-werewolves want her to set the record straight.
    E She is surprised that non-werewolves believe in werewolves.

Answer these questions about the way words and phrases are used in the text.

9 "Everybody thinks that werewolves are fairytale creatures, like unicorns or dragons, which is just ridiculous really" (lines 15-18). Which word in this sentence is a verb?

    A like
    B Everybody
    C ridiculous
    D thinks
    E werewolves

10 "interviews and TV appearances were crammed into my diary like sardines in a tin" (lines 42-44). This is an example of:

    A alliteration.
    B personification.
    C a metaphor.
    D a simile.
    E exaggeration.

Answer these questions about the meaning of words as they are used in the text.

11 The ideas that people have about werewolves are described as "ludicrous" (line 19).
What is meant by this?

- **A** They are dramatic and loud.
- **B** They are unusual and unhelpful.
- **C** They are sensible and funny.
- **D** They are boring and logical.
- **E** They are unreasonable and laughable.

12 What does the word "earnest" (line 31) mean?

- **A** Harsh
- **B** Insincere
- **C** Serious
- **D** Impatient
- **E** Indifferent

13 Which of these words is closest in meaning to "excluded" (line 59)?

- **A** Offended
- **B** Rejected
- **C** Unheard
- **D** Unkind
- **E** Tolerated

Turn over to the next page

Read this passage carefully and answer the questions that follow.

A Human Computer

Katherine Johnson was an African-American mathematician who worked at NASA (the National Aeronautics and Space Administration)

5   from the 1950s until the 1980s. During her pioneering career, she made an invaluable contribution to the US space programme and helped to break down some of the barriers faced by women and

10   African Americans in scientific fields.

Born in West Virginia in 1918, Johnson's talent for mathematics was apparent from a young age. She jumped several years ahead in school and by

15   the age of 15 she had begun studying at university. In 1937, when she was only 18, she graduated with degrees in mathematics and French. However, at that time, opportunities for women

20   and black people were severely limited because of widespread discrimination and segregation. For many years, Johnson had few chances to exercise her remarkable mathematical abilities.

25   Then, in 1953, Johnson found work as a "computer", supporting the work of the engineers who designed and built aircraft at the Langley Research Center. Johnson quickly stood out in her role thanks to her

30   insatiable thirst for knowledge — rather than just carrying out calculations, she always wanted to understand what she was working on as fully as possible. This inquisitiveness, coupled with her

35   determination, broke down barriers at Langley — women weren't traditionally allowed to attend the organisation's scientific meetings, but Johnson insisted on going to them, making it possible for

40   other women to attend too.

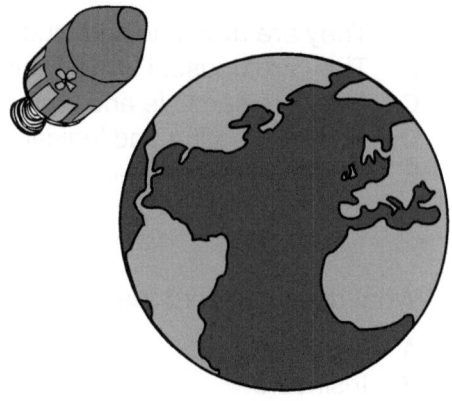

In the late 1950s, the USA began to focus on putting people into space, and Johnson joined the new Space Task Group which was set up to help achieve

45   this goal. Over the following years, she performed vital calculations for some of NASA's most celebrated missions, including the 1961 flight that took the first American, Alan Shepard, into space.

50   Shortly afterwards, Johnson was involved in calculating the flight path that allowed John Glenn to become the first American to orbit the Earth. By this point, NASA had begun using computing

55   machines to perform calculations, but these were prone to mistakes. Glenn only agreed to go ahead with his flight if Katherine Johnson checked the machine's numbers and confirmed that they were

60   correct.

For many decades, the significance of the contribution that Johnson and her fellow "computers" made to the US space programme was widely overlooked.

65   However, in recent years, they have received more recognition, and in 2016 they even became the subject of an Oscar-nominated film, with the rather appropriate title, *Hidden Figures*.

Answer these questions about the text. You can refer back to the text if you need to.
Pick the best answer and mark its letter on your answer sheet.

14 According to the text, why was it difficult for Johnson to find a job in her field?

    A She was not qualified to work in mathematics.
    B She could only work part-time.
    C Discrimination meant that she had limited opportunities.
    D She was too young to get a job in her field.
    E The space programme only began in the late 1950s.

15 When did Johnson become a "computer"?

    A 1918
    B 1937
    C 1953
    D 1961
    E 2016

16 According to the text, what was the role of the human "computers"?

    A To design and build aircraft
    B To assist astronauts with their work
    C To train engineers to build aircraft
    D To assist engineers with their work
    E To do the work of engineers

17 Johnson had an "insatiable thirst for knowledge" (line 30). This tells us that:

    A she was passionate about the work she was doing.
    B she was eager to show everyone what she knew.
    C she was proud of how much she had learnt.
    D she was reluctant to learn new things.
    E she was eager to learn new things.

18 According to the text, Johnson pushed boundaries at work by:

    A working harder than anyone else.
    B excelling in her role as a "computer".
    C using computing machines.
    D helping to send the first American into space.
    E participating in scientific meetings.

Turn over to the next page

19 John Glenn wanted Katherine Johnson to check the computing machine's calculations. This suggests that:

A he wanted her to do extra work.
B he thought that the calculations were easy.
C he had faith in her abilities.
D he wasn't allowed to check the calculations himself.
E he couldn't find anyone else to check the calculations.

20 According to the text, which statement about Johnson is not true?

A She stopped working for NASA in the 1980s.
B She studied more than one subject at university.
C She joined the Space Task Group when it was set up in the late 1950s.
D John Glenn's Earth orbit was the first NASA mission she worked on.
E She was born in West Virginia.

21 Why do you think the text calls "*Hidden Figures*" an "appropriate title" (line 69) for a film about the "computers"?

A Computing machines were given credit for work the "computers" did.
B The "computers" wanted to keep their work a secret.
C The "computers" didn't work on any well-known missions.
D The "computers" didn't work hard enough to be acknowledged.
E The importance of the work of the "computers" wasn't acknowledged for a long time.

Answer these questions about the meaning of words as they are used in the text.

22 Which of these words is closest in meaning to "pioneering" (line 6)?

A Trailblazing
B Traditional
C Famous
D Unusual
E Productive

23 The word "exercise" (line 23) could most accurately be replaced by:

A show off.
B perfect.
C employ.
D train.
E highlight.

Answer these questions about the way words and phrases are used in the text.

24 What type of words are these?

graduated   insisted   performed   confirmed

A Adjectives
B Verbs
C Adverbs
D Nouns
E Conjunctions

25 "For many years, Johnson had few chances to exercise her remarkable mathematical abilities" (lines 22-24). What type of word is "her" in this sentence?

A Preposition
B Verb
C Pronoun
D Determiner
E Noun

26 "Glenn only agreed to go ahead with his flight if Katherine Johnson checked the machine's numbers and confirmed that they were correct" (lines 56-60). Which word in this sentence is an adjective?

A with
B flight
C they
D confirmed
E correct

Turn over to the next page

This passage contains some spelling mistakes. Each numbered line has either one mistake or no mistake. For each line, work out which group of words contains a mistake and mark the letter on your answer sheet. Mark N if there is no mistake.

A Crafty Character

27 As the midday sun shone down on the hillside, Martin watched the mischevous llama

          A   B   C   D   N

28 enjoy a substansial mouthful of lush, green grass. This was the third time that Vivienne

          A   B   C   D   N

29 — a remarkably persistant creature — had managed to break out of the stables. It had

          A   B   C   D   N

30 taken Martin virtually the intire morning to find her, and he wasn't about to let her out of his

          A   B   C   D   N

31 sight now. Vivienne glared at him, aware that her new-found freedomn was in jeopardy.

          A   B   C   D   N

32 She let out a shriek and trotted father up the hillside towards the sheep, who were observing

          A   B   C   D   N

33 this unusual specticle curiously. Martin charged after her, but just as he got close enough

          A   B   C   D   N

34 to grab her, Vivienne turned and spat. Martin furiously wiped the saliva from his eyes, but

          A   B   C   D   N

it was too late — Vivienne had disappeared again.

This passage contains some mistakes involving capital letters and punctuation. Each numbered line has either one mistake or no mistake. For each line, work out which group of words contains a mistake and mark the letter on your answer sheet. Mark N if there is no mistake.

Diving with Sharks

35 If your'e tired of lounging around on the beach and feel the need for some excitement,
      A   B   C   D   N

36 then why not take the plunge on one of our shark experiences. Our qualified guides know
      A   B   C   D   N

37 all the best spots to get up close and personal with these remarkable creature's. While
      A   B   C   D   N

38 no previous diving experience is necessary — we do require customers to be confident
      A   B   C   D   N

39 swimming in deep water. Each experience includes; an introductory diving course,
      A   B   C   D   N

40 a one-hour dive and a delicious fish dinner on the boat before you head back to shore.
      A   B   C   D   N

41 So instead of settling down on that lounger for the umpteenth time give us a call or visit
      A   B   C   D   N

42 our Website to discover the "jawsome" adventures that await in our shark-infested waters.
      A   B   C   D   N

Turn over to the next page

For each numbered line, choose the word, or group of words, which completes the passage correctly. The passage needs to make sense and be written in correct English. Pick one of the five options and mark the letter on your answer sheet.

Haircut from Hell

43 Normally, Ishani loved **absolutely** **entirely** **completely** **wholly** **certainly** everything
          A   B   C   D   E

44 about having her hair cut. **Sat** **Seated** **Sitting** **Was sitting** **To sit** in the stylist's chair
                                  A   B   C   D   E

45 was one of the few occasions **that** **who** **which** **whom** **when** she could take time out
                                     A   B   C   D   E

46 and really unwind. **Yesterday** **Last week** **Today** **Tomorrow** **Later** though, Ishani
                            A   B   C   D   E

47 could not relax **due to** **whereas** **owing to** **because** **on account of** the salon
                         A   B   C   D   E

48 experience was rapidly becoming her **greatest** **baddest** **worse** **most great** **largest**
                                            A   B   C   D   E

49 nightmare. With just a few clumsy cuts, her **fixed** **usual** **average** **general** **daily**
                                                     A   B   C   D   E

50 flowing hairstyle had somehow been transformed **to** **in** **on** **from** **into** a tangled pile
                                                        A   B   C   D   E

of clippings at her feet.

End of Test

11+ English

For Ages 10-11
Practice Paper 8

For GL Assessment

Read the following:

Do not open this booklet or start the test until you are told to do so.

1. This is a multiple-choice test.

2. There are 50 questions and you will have 50 minutes to do the test.

3. You should mark your answer to each question in pencil on the separate answer sheet.

4. You should only mark one answer for each question. To mark your answer,
    draw a straight line through the rectangle next to the option you have chosen.
    If you make a mistake, rub it out and mark your new answer clearly.

5. Make sure you keep your place on the answer sheet and mark your
    answer in the box that has the same number as the question.

6. Do as many questions as you can. If you get stuck on a question, choose the answer
    that you think is most likely to be correct, then move on to the next question.

7. You should do any rough working on a separate piece of paper.

Work carefully, but go as quickly as you can.

Read this passage carefully and answer the questions that follow.

In Search of a Friend

"Evie, Evie, look at this!" Ben shouted, bursting through the front door. He waved a brightly coloured leaflet at his sister. "There's a competition for students to
5 build the best robot. We have to enter!"

Intrigued, Evie took the leaflet and studied it. Bold letters were emblazoned across the top of the paper: "Build Best Bot and Win £5000". The competition was
10 open to all school students in the town, and they had three months to design and build their robot.

"£5000! Just imagine what we could do with that," Evie said.

15 Finding an original idea was the first obstacle, and it seemed almost insurmountable: you could hardly move without bumping into a robot nowadays. In shops, restaurants, schools and taxis,
20 robots assisted humans with their jobs. Even in people's houses, an army of trusty robots tackled all the tedious chores that most people were so averse to. Evie and Ben's own household robot arrived in
25 the hallway then, wearing his usual blank expression.

"Evie Wilson. Ben Wilson. Good afternoon," Cyd droned. "Can I take your things?"

30 "Thanks, Cyd," Evie said to the robot with a smile. "How was your day?"

"Satisfactory," Cyd replied curtly. Evie rolled her eyes. Sometimes she wasn't sure why she made so much effort to be
35 polite to Cyd. She knew that he couldn't help the way he was programmed, but she wished she could live with a robot who had more flair for conversation.

"Ben," she said suddenly. "I think I've
40 got it! We should make a robot who can help you by being your friend."

"That's a great idea," her brother replied. "I can't believe nobody's ever thought of it before. It could be a real
45 comfort to lonely people."

The siblings were so captivated by their idea that neither of them noticed Cyd reverse forlornly from the room.

Dinner was barely over that night
50 when Evie and Ben set about sketching plans for their robot. All sorts of different designs piled up around them as they worked, trying to come up with a robot that would be more than just an impersonal
55 automaton. Both children excelled at robotics, but they realised that the programming would be more complicated than anything they'd attempted before. It was no easy task to bestow human
60 qualities on a machine.

Finally, after several weeks of painstaking work and innumerable false starts, they settled on a design that they thought might work. Their robot would
65 be compact and smooth, encased in shiny metal — Evie maintained that humanoid robots looked creepy. It would be programmed to recognise facial expressions and react appropriately. They
70 only planned to tackle happiness and sadness at first, but they could always

expand its repertoire later. Although this would be a huge challenge, they were both so eager to see their robot materialise that neither of them felt daunted by the project.

Just a couple of days after they started building their robot, however, their carefully crafted design vanished. Evie and Ben ransacked their rooms for it and even enlisted their parents' help. It was nowhere to be seen. When they asked Cyd, he gave his programmed reply: "I will do my best to assist you, Evie Wilson and Ben Wilson."

The next morning, the design reappeared. The siblings were so relieved that they didn't stop to think about where it had been. With just under two months until the competition deadline, they still had a mountain of work to do to make sure that their robot was ready in time. They buried themselves away in Evie's room whenever they had a free moment, emerging at mealtimes with tired eyes and satisfied smiles.

Their robot advanced a little more each day, despite the occasional setback when things went missing again — one day it was their favourite screwdriver, another it was Ben's copy of the textbook that they were using to check their code. Luckily, they could usually find a suitable replacement for the things that went astray.

The closer the deadline loomed, the faster time slipped away and the more frequently things disappeared. By this stage, the missing items were largely redundant, but when the metal casing that would form their robot's outer shell took flight one week before the competition, they began to despair.

After unsuccessfully combing the entire house, Evie and Ben headed to Cyd's cupboard to ask for his help. Ben opened the door and stopped in his tracks, his eyes as wide as saucers. Cyd's cupboard was a pirate's cave, crammed with stolen treasure. Tools and paper were stacked in the gloomy corners and, glinting in the dim light of Cyd's glowing eyes, was the robot's casing.

"Cyd, what's all this?" Evie demanded.

"I am sorry," Cyd replied eventually, his electronic brain struggling to find the unfamiliar words. "I know I should not have taken your things. I thought that if you could not make your robot then you would let me be your friend."

"Oh, Cyd," Evie and Ben cried as guilt washed over them. They'd been so focused on their project that they had been completely oblivious to Cyd's feelings about their new creation. It had never occurred to them that humans might not be the only ones to experience loneliness.

"You're already our friend," Ben said, offering the robot a reassuring smile. "This new robot can't change that."

"In fact," Evie said, "why don't you help us finish building our robot? We'd love your help, and then it can be friends with all of us."

For the first time, Cyd's impassive digital expression transformed into something resembling a smile.

"I would like that, Evie Wilson and Ben Wilson," he said. "I would like that very much."

Turn over to the next page

Answer these questions about the text. You can refer back to the text if you need to. Pick the best answer and mark its letter on your answer sheet.

1 According to the text, which of the following details does not appear on the leaflet?

   A Who can enter the competition
   B When the results will be announced
   C The goal of the competition
   D The competition prize
   E The competition deadline

2 What is the first challenge that Evie and Ben face when they decide to enter the competition?

   A Drawing a design for the robot
   B Deciding on a name for the robot
   C Programming the robot
   D Coming up with an idea for the robot
   E Buying the materials to make the robot

3 The text does not mention robots that help in the workplace of:

   A taxi drivers.
   B teachers.
   C shop assistants.
   D chefs.
   E postal workers.

4 Robots do all the chores that people are "averse to" (line 23). This tells us that:

   A people think household chores aren't their responsibility.
   B people are unable to do household chores.
   C people complain about doing household chores.
   D people are too busy to do household chores.
   E people dislike doing household chores.

5 Cyd arrives in the hallway "wearing his usual blank expression" (lines 25-26). This suggests that:

   A Cyd doesn't show any emotions.
   B Cyd doesn't have any facial features.
   C Cyd is in a bad mood.
   D Cyd finds his job boring.
   E Cyd doesn't like the children.

6 Which of the following first inspires Evie's idea for their robot?

A She wants a robot that is more talkative.
B She feels lonely.
C She wants to help lonely people.
D She wants to spend the prize money.
E She likes to do things that have never been done before.

7 Which adjective best describes Ben's attitude to Evie's idea for their robot?

A Apprehensive
B Shocked
C Excited
D Distracted
E Embarrassed

8 Why do you think Cyd left the room when he heard the children's idea?

A He was angry.
B He was unhappy.
C He wanted to help.
D He was happy.
E He wasn't interested.

9 Which detail best shows that Evie and Ben were eager to start work on their robot?

A They ignored Cyd leaving the room.
B They spent a long time on their design.
C They began straight after dinner.
D They worked on the robot in their free time.
E They were happy when their lost design reappeared.

10 "All sorts of different designs piled up around them as they worked" (lines 51-53).
Why do you think the author added this detail?

A To show that the children are messy.
B To show that the children are bad at robotics.
C To show that the children are lazy.
D To show that the children want their design to be perfect.
E To show that the children don't have many ideas.

Turn over to the next page

5

11 How long did it take the children to decide on a design for their robot?

    A   A couple of days
    B   One week
    C   Several weeks
    D   Two months
    E   Three months

12 According to the text, which of the following is not part of the children's design for their robot?

    A   It will be small.
    B   It will be humanoid.
    C   It will be smooth.
    D   It will be made of metal.
    E   It will be shiny.

13 According to the text, what will the children's robot be able to do?

    A   Make people laugh
    B   Give people hugs
    C   Identify every emotion
    D   Recognise facial expressions
    E   Recognise people by their faces

14 Why do you think Evie and Ben "didn't stop to think" (line 88) about where their design had been?

    A   They didn't mind losing their design.
    B   They already had a new design.
    C   They knew where their design had gone.
    D   They were completely focused on building the robot.
    E   They had memorised their design.

15 Where do Evie and Ben build their robot?

    A In the hallway
    B At school
    C In Ben's bedroom
    D In Cyd's cupboard
    E In Evie's bedroom

16 Which of the following items did not go missing while the children were building their robot?

    A A screwdriver
    B The design
    C A textbook
    D A computer
    E The metal casing

17 How do Evie and Ben feel when the final item goes missing?

    A Guilty
    B Hopeless
    C Furious
    D Worried
    E Irritated

18 Why do you think Evie asked Cyd to help them finish building their robot?

    A To stop him taking their things
    B To help them finish the robot more quickly
    C To make him feel jealous
    D To make him feel included
    E Because he knew a lot about robots

Turn over to the next page

Answer these questions about the meaning of words as they are used in the text.

19 What does the word "tedious" (line 22) mean?
  A Difficult
  B Endless
  C Tiresome
  D Relentless
  E Unappealing

20 The word "ransacked" (line 80) could most accurately be replaced by:
  A searched.
  B attacked.
  C inquired.
  D studied.
  E analysed.

21 Which of the following is closest in meaning to "emerging" (line 95)?
  A Departing
  B Coming out
  C Combining
  D Going in
  E Developing

22 Which of these words is closest in meaning to "reassuring" (line 140)?
  A Tender
  B Sincere
  C Friendly
  D Comforting
  E Cheerful

Answer these questions about the way words and phrases are used in the text.

23 The phrase "Build Best Bot" (lines 8-9) is an example of:

    A onomatopoeia.
    B alliteration.
    C a simile.
    D a homophone.
    E a metaphor.

24 "an army of trusty robots tackled all the tedious chores" (lines 21-22).
What type of word is "army" in this sentence?

    A Abstract noun
    B Possessive pronoun
    C Relative pronoun
    D Collective noun
    E Proper noun

25 Which of the following sentences includes a metaphor?

    A "Intrigued, Evie took the leaflet and studied it."
    B "Sometimes she wasn't sure why she made so much effort to be polite to Cyd."
    C "It was no easy task to bestow human qualities on a machine."
    D "Ben opened the door and stopped in his tracks, his eyes as wide as saucers."
    E "Cyd's cupboard was a pirate's cave, crammed with stolen treasure."

26 What type of words are these?

    impersonal   occasional   redundant   electronic

    A Adverbs
    B Nouns
    C Verbs
    D Conjunctions
    E Adjectives

Turn over to the next page

This passage contains some spelling mistakes. Each numbered line has either one mistake or no mistake. For each line, work out which group of words contains a mistake and mark the letter on your answer sheet. Mark N if there is no mistake.

Cutlery Crook Caught

27 After a painstaking investigation, the mastermined behind a recent spate of cutlery thefts in

    A   B   C   D   N

28 Forkstone has finally been tracked down. Beaky, a malitious magpie from Forkstone park,

    A   B   C   D   N

29 was caught red-handed on Wednesday mourning by Nadeem, a retired social worker

    A   B   C   D   N

30 and avid bird watcher. Local residents were stunned to hear that the crafty criminal had

    A   B   C   D   N

31 been sneaking into kitchens thoroughout Forkstone in search of shiny silverware, and had

    A   B   C   D   N

32 amassed a collection of over one hundred spoons, knives and forks. Police are urgeing

    A   B   C   D   N

33 residents to remain vigilant, as it is possible that Beaky had an accomplice. All the stolen

    A   B   C   D   N

34 pieces of cutlery are expected to be returned to their writeful owners within a few days.

    A   B   C   D   N

This passage contains some mistakes involving capital letters and punctuation. Each numbered line has either one mistake or no mistake. For each line, work out which group of words contains a mistake and mark the letter on your answer sheet. Mark N if there is no mistake.

Picture Perfect

35 Roisin sat patiently in the hallway, she was waiting to be called into the drawing room.
       A   B   C   D   N

36 To say she was apprehensive was an understatement. A month ago, Lord Nimbleton —
       A   B   C   D   N

37 a very wealthy and notoriously thin-skinned gentleman had tasked her with painting his
       A   B   C   D   N

38 portrait. Lord N (as he liked to be called) was a dignified man with tiny grey eyes teeth
       A   B   C   D   N

39 that a horse would be proud of and ears that could rival an african elephant's. Accurately
       A   B   C   D   N

40 recreating Nimbleton's highly distinctive appearance on canvas had been no mean feat.
       A   B   C   D   N

41 "Good morning Miss McCrawley" Lord N boomed. "Shall we take a look at this splendid
       A   B   C   D   N

42 portrait of yours?" I can't tell you how much I've been looking forward to seeing it."
       A   B   C   D   N

Turn over to the next page

For each numbered line, choose the word, or group of words, which completes the passage correctly. The passage needs to make sense and be written in correct English. Pick one of the five options and mark the letter on your answer sheet.

How to Make a Pompom

43 Take a piece of cardboard and cut **through out down on into** two 8 cm-wide circles.

                                                A B C D E

44 Cut a slit from the edge to the middle of **each every this that some** circle

                                                A B C D E

and then carefully cut a 2 cm hole in the centre of both circles. Sandwich the circles

45 together and wrap wool around them, **pass passed passes passage passing** it

                                                A B C D E

46 through the central hole. **Implant Input Inside Insert Invert** scissors between the

                                                A B C D E

47 circles and cut through the wool **totally fully all wholly utterly** the way around.

                                                A B C D E

48 Next, slip a length of wool **amid towards during about between** the cardboard

                                                A B C D E

49 circles, wrap it around your pompom and tie it — this **might can will may could**

                                                A B C D E

50 hold the pompom together. **In conclusion Finally At last Eventually Ultimately,**

                                                A B C D E

remove the cardboard circles, and your pompom is finished.

End of Test

11+ English

For **GL** Assessment

Practice Paper Answer Book

Ages 10-11

Pack 2

Paper 5

1) B

'impressive' means the same as "magnificent", and 'colourful' means the same as "vibrant".

2) E

Lines 22-24 state that "Deconstructing the towers" is "often a more perilous" part of the display than constructing them.

3) B

Line 34 states that one of the functions of the sash is to provide "back support" for the *castellers*.

4) C

Lines 45-46 state that the "shared values" of the tradition help to "foster a sense of solidarity", but 'solidarity' is not given as one of the values.

5) C

Lines 56-58 state that the teams receive marks for the "height" of their tower and for their "construction technique", which means the method they use.

6) C

If something is "heart-stopping", it means it is thrilling.

7) D

Lines 7-8 give the English for *castell*. Lines 13-14 mention how many levels *castells* can have. Lines 17-18 state that music is played. Line 52 states how often the tournament happens. The number of people involved in making a single *castell* is not mentioned.

8) C

You would be most likely to find this text in a travel guide because it describes a cultural tradition in a foreign country.

9) A

"apex" means 'the top' or 'the highest point'.

10) B

'encourage' is closest in meaning to "foster" in the sense that both words are to do with supporting the development of something.

11) D

"a remarkable display" is the subject because it is doing the action of the sentence.

12) A

These words are abstract nouns because they are ideas rather than things you can see, touch, hear, smell or taste.

13) D

"crowd" is a verb because it is one of the action words in the sentence.

14) C

In lines 7-8, Aaliyah says that the rumours about ghostly activity are "complete nonsense". This shows that she thinks the ghostly activity doesn't really happen.

15) A

If you drag your feet, you deliberately walk slowly. Imran deliberately walks slowly because he is apprehensive about entering the old library.

16) D

If you take great delight in something, you enjoy doing it. Imran's friends liked to tease Imran by telling him "terrifying tales" about the old library.

17) C

Lines 24-27 state that curtains "obscured" the windows, only letting "a few slivers of light" into the room. Lines 31-32 state that when Aaliyah switched on the light, "nothing happened".

18) E

If something is "fitting", it means that it is appropriate. The graveyard is described as a "fitting view" because the description of it in lines 35-37 gives you the impression that it is a spooky place, just like the old library.

19) D

Lines 44-45 state that the tapping sound is "muffled to begin with", which means that it was quiet at first. Then it slowly "became louder".

20) B

Lines 53-54 state that Aaliyah took "a few tentative steps" in the direction of the tapping sound. "tentative" means uncertain or cautious, so this shows that Aaliyah moved towards the sound hesitantly.

21) B

The phrase "bolted for the door" means that Aaliyah rushed towards the door. This shows that she wanted to leave the room quickly.

22) E

This is personification because the shelves are given human qualities.

23) C

These words are adjectives because they describe nouns.

24) D

'run-down' is closest in meaning to "dilapidated" because both words describe something that is old and in poor condition.

25) A

You can replace "cascaded" with the word 'tumbled' because they both mean the books poured onto the floor.

26) C

"sprightly" means that the cat was full of energy.

27) C

'extrordinary' should be 'extraordinary' — it is a compound word.

28) B

'exageration' should be 'exaggeration' — the root word is 'exaggerate'.

29) B

'recieved' should be 'received' — you need to use the 'i' before 'e' rule.

30) N

There are no mistakes in this line.

31) A

'whether' should be 'weather'. These words are homophones — they sound the same, but are spelt differently.

32) B

'incredably' should be 'incredibly' — the root word is 'incredible'.

33) C

'perswade' should be 'persuade' — the 'w' sound is spelt 'u'.

34) C

'profesional' should be 'professional' — the root word is 'profession'.

2

35) B
There should be a comma or a full stop after 'forlornly' — punctuation is needed between the reporting clause and the direct speech.

36) B
'wasnt' needs an apostrophe (wasn't) because it is a shortened version of 'was not'.

37) D
There should not be a comma after 'and'.

38) D
'sludge' should be followed by a full stop to complete the sentence.

39) A
There should be a comma or an exclamation mark after 'stuck' — direct speech always ends with a punctuation mark inside the inverted commas.

40) D
There should be a comma after 'grip' to separate the fronted adverbial from the rest of the sentence.

41) C
The apostrophe in 'Tims' should be before the 's' (Tim's) to show singular possession.

42) N
There are no mistakes in this line.

43) B
'origins' is correct because it is the noun that makes the most sense in the context of the passage.

44) A
'The' is the determiner that makes the most sense in the context of the sentence.

45) D
'taught' is correct because the sentence is written in the passive voice.

46) C
'within' is the preposition that makes the most sense.

47) A
'although' is the correct conjunction because it introduces a statement that contrasts with the previous clause.

48) E
'higher' is correct because it is a comparative adjective.

49) A
'has spread' is correct, as the present perfect form of the verb shows that it has already happened.

50) C
'emergence' is correct because it is the correct spelling of the noun.

Paper 6

1) B
Line 3 states that palm oil is "extracted from the fruit of the oil palm tree".

2) E
Lines 8-9 list products containing palm oil — chocolate is not mentioned.

3) C
Lines 10-12 state that "palm oil now accounts for 40% of vegetable oil consumption worldwide".

4) D
Lines 22-24 state that palm oil gives foods "a longer shelf life" and that it stops ice cream from "melting too quickly".

5) D
Line 28 states that tallow is "animal fat", which means it comes from animals.

6) E
Lines 35-36 mention that there was a "trend for more plant-based ingredients", which means customers wanted more plant-based ingredients in their products.

7) D
Lines 61-63 state that "oil palm trees use less land than other oil-producing crops".

8) B
Lines 55-60 state that the world's population will be larger in the future, so we need to "make sure that there will be enough food for everyone".

9) E
If something is controversial, people disagree about it. People might disagree about palm oil production because of the "disadvantages" described in lines 73-100.

10) A
Lines 77-78 state that Indonesia and Malaysia "produce around 85% of the world's palm oil".

11) E
Lines 81-83 state that cutting down trees "releases lots of greenhouse gases (like carbon dioxide) into the atmosphere".

12) B
In the text it says that orangutans and tigers are "already in danger" (line 91) because of other factors and that palm oil is "adding to the threats" (line 87) they face. Therefore, palm oil production is not the main threat.

13) B
Lines 106-107 state that palm oil production is predicted to "increase by more than 300% in the next three decades".

14) D
If something is detrimental, it is harmful, so the phrase means 'causing harm to the environment'.

15) C
Lines 114-115 mention that the RSPO is trying to encourage palm oil production "without deforestation".

16) A
Lines 124-129 state that the wildlife corridors in Malaysia will "connect isolated patches of forest together" to give animals "safe pathways" between forested areas.

3

17)   D

The last paragraph of the text states that some companies are "reluctant" to switch to sustainable palm oil because it "costs more to produce".

18)   E

Line 4 states that oil palm trees come from Africa. Lines 31-34 mention that tallow was used in foods and beauty products. Lines 104-107 predict that palm oil production will increase in the future. Lines 115-116 state that 20% of palm oil is RSPO certified. The text does not mention how to tell if palm oil is from a sustainable source.

19)   C

'produce' is closest in meaning to "generate" in the sense that palm oil helps local communities to make money.

20)   B

"dwindling" means that the forests are 'shrinking' in size.

21)   D

If something is "booming", it is flourishing, so this means that the palm oil industry is very successful.

22)   E

You can replace "reluctant" with the word 'unwilling' because they both describe not wanting to do something.

23)   A

"standard" is an adjective in this sentence because it describes the noun "addition".

24)   D

These words are adverbs because they are used to describe verbs or adjectives.

25)   A

"which" is a relative pronoun in this sentence — it refers back to the noun phrase "Malaysia's elephants".

26)   B

"more" is a determiner in this sentence because it tells you how much work there is.

27)   A

'rumaged' should be 'rummaged' — it has a double consonant after a short vowel, like 'summer' or 'plummet'.

28)   A

'prefered' should be 'preferred' — when you add a suffix beginning with a vowel to a word ending with 'fer', you have to double the 'r' if the 'fer' part of the word is stressed.

29)   B

'insident' should be 'incident'.

30)   N

There are no mistakes in this line.

31)   B

'disobediant' should be 'disobedient' — the root word is 'obedient'.

32)   C

'atending' should be 'attending' — it has a double consonant after a short vowel, like 'attempt' or 'attract'.

33)   B

'calender' should be 'calendar'.

34)   B

'siezed' should be 'seized' — it is an exception to the 'i' before 'e' rule.

35)   B

'tuesday' should have a capital letter because it is a proper noun.

36)   D

The word 'ago' should be followed by a comma to separate the extra information in the sentence.

37)   C

'it's' should be 'its' because it shows possession, rather than a shortened version of 'it is'.

38)   A

There should be a bracket after 'John' to complete the pair.

39)   C

'Said' should not have a capital letter because it is not at the start of a sentence.

40)   B

The comma after 'do' should be a colon because it is introducing a list.

41)   D

There should be a semi-colon after 'cheese' to separate the items in the list.

42)   D

There should be inverted commas after the full stop to end the direct speech.

43)   E

'another' is the word that makes the most sense.

44)   C

'at' is the preposition that makes the most sense in this sentence.

45)   B

'Where' is correct because it is the question word that makes the most sense in this sentence.

46)   C

'waves' is correct because there's no article before the adjective 'towering', so you need a plural noun.

47)   A

'endless' is correct because it fits with the following word 'weeks' — the other options can't describe the noun 'weeks'.

48)   B

'just' is correct because it completes the phrase 'just about to'.

49)   E

'and' correctly links together the statements about what Poppy was going to do — it shows that she was going to have a nap after going below.

50)   C

'had been' is correct because it is the present perfect form of 'to be'. It shows that the black flag was spotted before the shout from the crow's nest.

4

Paper 7

1) **E**
Lines 2-3 state that Saffie "only wrote the essay in the first place as a homework assignment".

2) **B**
"monumental" is closest in meaning to 'important'.

3) **C**
Lines 25-27 state that "the only thing that the stories get right is that we transform during a full moon".

4) **A**
Line 28 states that journalists find Saffie disappointing because they have "false expectations" about her. This shows that she doesn't conform to the stereotypes about werewolves.

5) **E**
If something strikes a chord, its means that it causes sympathy or emotion, so the essay made people feel sympathy for Saffie.

6) **E**
Line 46 states that Saffie finds her media appearances "exhilarating", which means the same as 'exciting'. Line 47 mentions that the media attention can be "exhausting", which means the same as 'tiring'.

7) **C**
In lines 48-50, Saffie says "it looks like all this attention is sparking some real change for werewolves", which suggests she feels optimistic about the future for werewolves.

8) **B**
In lines 56-58, Saffie says that "a surprising number" of the non-werewolves who have contacted her say they can "relate" to her story.

9) **D**
"thinks" is a verb because it is one of the action words in this sentence.

10) **D**
Similes compare two different things and have the word 'like' or 'as' in them, so "crammed into my diary <u>like</u> sardines in a tin" is a simile.

11) **E**
The word "ludicrous" means 'ridiculous'. Saffie thinks that the ideas are unreasonable and laughable.

12) **C**
The word "earnest" means 'serious' or sincere. The interviewer used a serious tone of voice when he asked Saffie whether she eats humans.

13) **B**
'rejected' is closest in meaning to "excluded" because both words can mean 'left out'.

14) **C**
Lines 19-21 state that "opportunities for women and black people were severely limited because of widespread discrimination".

15) **C**
Lines 25-26 state that Johnson found work as a "computer" in 1953.

16) **D**
Lines 26-27 state that Johnson was "supporting the work of the engineers" at the Langley Research Center.

17) **E**
Having an "insatiable thirst" for something means having a very strong desire for it, so Johnson was eager to learn new things.

18) **E**
Lines 35-40 state that Johnson "broke down barriers" by attending scientific meetings that women weren't usually allowed to go to.

19) **C**
The fact that John Glenn wanted Johnson to check the machine's calculations suggests that he had more faith in her abilities than in the machine.

20) **D**
Before she assisted with the calculations for John Glenn's Earth orbit, she was involved in "the 1961 flight that took the first American, Alan Shepard, into space" (lines 48-49).

21) **E**
Lines 61-64 state that "the significance of the contribution" that the "computers" made was "widely overlooked" for "many decades", which means the work of these 'figures' on the space programme could be described as 'hidden'.

22) **A**
'trailblazing' is closest in meaning to "pioneering" because both words can be used to describe things that have never been done before.

23) **C**
The word "exercise" could be replaced by 'employ' because both words can mean 'to make use of'.

24) **B**
These words are verbs because they are action words.

25) **D**
"her" is a determiner in this sentence because it shows that the "mathematical abilities" belong to Katherine Johnson.

26) **E**
"correct" is an adjective because it describes the noun "numbers".

27) **D**
'mischevous' should be 'mischievous' — the root word is 'mischief'.

28) **A**
'substansial' should be 'substantial' — the ending should be 'tial'.

29) **A**
'persistant' should be 'persistent' — the ending should be 'ent'.

30) **B**
'intire' should be 'entire'.

31) **C**
'freedomn' should be 'freedom' — there is no silent 'n' in the word.

32) **B**
'father' should be 'farther'. These words are homophones — they sound the same but are spelt differently.

33) **A**
'specticle' should be 'spectacle' — the ending should be 'acle'.

34) **N**
There are no mistakes in this line.

35) **A**
'your'e' should be 'you're' — the apostrophe shows that it is a shortened version of 'you are'.

36) **C**
There should be a question mark after 'experiences' instead of a full stop.

37) **D**
'creature's' doesn't need an apostrophe because it is a plural noun.

5

38) B
The dash between 'necessary' and 'we' should be a comma to separate the subordinate clause from the main clause.

39) C
There shouldn't be a semi-colon after 'includes'.

40) N
There are no mistakes in this line.

41) C
There should be a comma after 'time' to separate the subordinate clause from the main clause.

42) A
'Website' shouldn't have a capital letter because it isn't a proper noun.

43) A
'absolutely' is the correct adverb because it makes the most sense in the context of the passage.

44) C
'Sitting' is correct because it's the option that makes the most sense in this sentence.

45) E
'when' is the correct relative pronoun because it introduces a relative clause that refers back to 'occasions' when Ishani could 'unwind'.

46) C
'Today' is correct because it makes sense with the verb, which is in the past progressive form (was becoming).

47) D
'because' is correct because it's the conjunction that makes the most sense in this sentence.

48) A
'greatest' is correct because it is the only option that is both spelt correctly and makes sense in this sentence.

49) B
'usual' is correct because it completes the noun phrase 'her usual flowing hairstyle'.

50) E
'into' is the correct preposition because it makes the most sense in this sentence.

Paper 8

1) B
Line 10 states that the competition is open to "all school students in the town". Lines 8-9 state that the goal of the competition is to build the best robot. Line 9 states that the prize is "£5000". Line 11 states that entrants have "three months" to complete their robot. The only piece of information not given is when the result will be announced.

2) D
Lines 15-16 state that coming up with an idea was "the first obstacle".

3) E
Line 19 mentions robots helping in "shops, restaurants, schools and taxis" — the passage doesn't mention robots helping in the workplace of postal workers.

4) E
If you are "averse to" something, you don't like it, so this means that people dislike doing household chores.

5) A
If you have a "blank expression", it means that you aren't showing any emotion. Cyd usually has a "blank expression", which suggests that he doesn't show any emotions.

6) A
Line 38 states that Evie is thinking about what it would be like to have a robot with "more flair for conversation" when she first comes up with the idea for their robot.

7) C
In line 42, Ben says that Evie's suggestion is "a great idea" and line 46 mentions that the children were "captivated" by the concept.

8) B
Line 48 states that Cyd left the room "forlornly", and 'forlorn' means 'unhappy'.

9) C
Line 49 states that "Dinner was barely over" when the children started to plan their robot, which shows that they wanted to get started as soon as possible.

10) D
This shows that the children worked hard to refine their design and come up with something as good as possible.

11) C
Lines 61-62 state that the children settled on a design "after several weeks of painstaking work".

12) B
The robot would not be humanoid because "Evie maintained that humanoid robots looked creepy" (lines 66-67).

13) D
Lines 68-69 state that the robot will be "programmed to recognise facial expressions".

14) D
If you don't stop to think about something, it suggests that you are completely focused on something else. The children didn't stop to think about where the design had been because they were completely focused on building the robot.

15) E
Lines 93-94 state that the children "buried themselves away in Evie's room".

6

16) D

As well as the design for the robot, the text mentions "their favourite screwdriver", "Ben's copy of the textbook" and "the metal casing" going missing.

17) B

Line 113 states that the children "began to despair" when the robot's casing disappeared. This means that they felt hopeless about the situation.

18) D

Evie and Ben feel "guilt" (line 132) that they didn't notice Cyd was feeling lonely, and Evie says that if Cyd helps with the robot, it "can be friends with all of us" (lines 144-145). This shows that she wants Cyd to feel included.

19) C

'tiresome' is closest in meaning to "tedious" because both words can be used to describe something that is boring.

20) A

You can replace "ransacked" with 'searched' because they both mean 'to look for something'.

21) B

'coming out' is closest in meaning to "emerging". The children come out of Evie's room at mealtimes.

22) D

'comforting' is closest in meaning to "reassuring" because both words are to do with making someone feel less worried about something.

23) B

The repeated 'b' sound in "Build Best Bot" is an example of alliteration.

24) D

"army" is a collective noun because it refers to a group of robots.

25) E

Metaphors describe something by saying that it is something else, so "Cyd's cupboard was a pirate's cave" is a metaphor.

26) E

These words are adjectives because they are words which describe nouns.

27) B

'mastermined' should be 'mastermind'.

28) C

'malitious' should be 'malicious' — the ending should be 'cious'.

29) B

'mourning' should be 'morning'. These words are homophones — they sound the same, but are spelt differently.

30) N

There are no mistakes in this line.

31) B

'thoroughout' should be 'throughout' — there is no 'o' before the 'r'.

32) D

'urgeing' should be 'urging' — you drop the 'e' when you add the suffix 'ing'.

33) B

'vigilent' should be 'vigilant' — the ending should be 'ant'.

34) C

'writeful' should be 'rightful' — the root word is 'right'.

35) B

The comma after 'hallway' should be a colon. Colons can join two main clauses together.

36) N

There are no mistakes in this line.

37) C

There should be a dash after 'gentleman' to separate the extra information in the sentence.

38) D

There should be a comma after 'eyes' to separate the items in the list.

39) C

'african' should have a capital letter because it comes from the proper noun 'Africa'.

40) N

There are no mistakes in this line.

41) B

There should be a comma or an exclamation mark after 'McCrawley'. Direct speech always ends with a punctuation mark inside the inverted commas.

42) A

There shouldn't be inverted commas after the question mark because Lord Nimbleton hasn't finished speaking.

43) B

'out' is correct because it completes the phrasal verb 'cut out', which makes the most sense in this sentence.

44) A

'each' is the correct determiner because the sentence refers to both of the pieces of cardboard.

45) E

'passing' is the form of the verb 'to pass' that makes sense in this sentence.

46) D

'Insert' is the correct verb to describe putting the scissors between the circles.

47) C

'all' is correct because it completes the phrase 'all the way'.

48) E

'between' is the preposition that makes the most sense in this sentence.

49) C

'will' is the correct modal verb because it indicates certainty rather than possibility.

50) B

'Finally' is correct because it begins a sentence which describes the last step in the process.

0524 - 29116

11+ English

For **GL** Assessment

Practice Paper
Answer Sheets

Ages
10-11

Pack 2

BLANK PAGE

2

Using the Multiple Choice Answer Sheets

If you're doing a Multiple Choice paper, it's often marked by a computer. These papers use special answer sheets like the ones in this booklet.

There's a Multiple Choice answer sheet to go with each Practice Paper, so make sure you're filling in the right one. If you get used to these answer sheets now, it means there'll be no nasty surprises when you sit the real test.

Here are a few tips for using the answer sheets without getting yourself in a pickle...

Tips for Filling in the Answer Sheets

1) Before you start, fill in your name and the name of your school in the correct space. There may be boxes for other information, like your date of birth or your pupil number. Make sure you don't leave anything blank by mistake.

2) To mark your answer, put a clear pencil line through the answer box.

3) Make sure you have a pencil sharpener and an eraser for any mistakes.

4) If you make a mistake, rub out the incorrect answer first, and then fill in your new answer clearly.

5) It's easy to lose your place when you move from the practice paper to the answer sheet, so match up the question number on the paper and the answer sheet. Keeping the two sheets close together will help you do this.

6) If you skip a question to come back to later, make sure you leave a gap for that question on the answer sheet. That way your answers will stay in order.

7) Don't do rough working on your answer sheet.

8) Don't worry if you put the same letter several times in a row — just because you've put 'B' four times, it doesn't mean that your answers are wrong.

English Practice Paper 5

Pupil's name:		Test date:

School name:

Please mark like this: ⊢─┤

Paper 5

Pupil Number

School Number

Date of Birth

Day	Month	Year
[0] [0]	January	2005
[1] [1]	February	2006
[2] [2]	March	2007
[3] [3]	April	2008
[4]	May	2009
[5]	June	2010
[6]	July	2011
[7]	August	2012
[8]	September	2013
[9]	October	2014
	November	2015
	December	2016

The *Castellers* of Catalonia

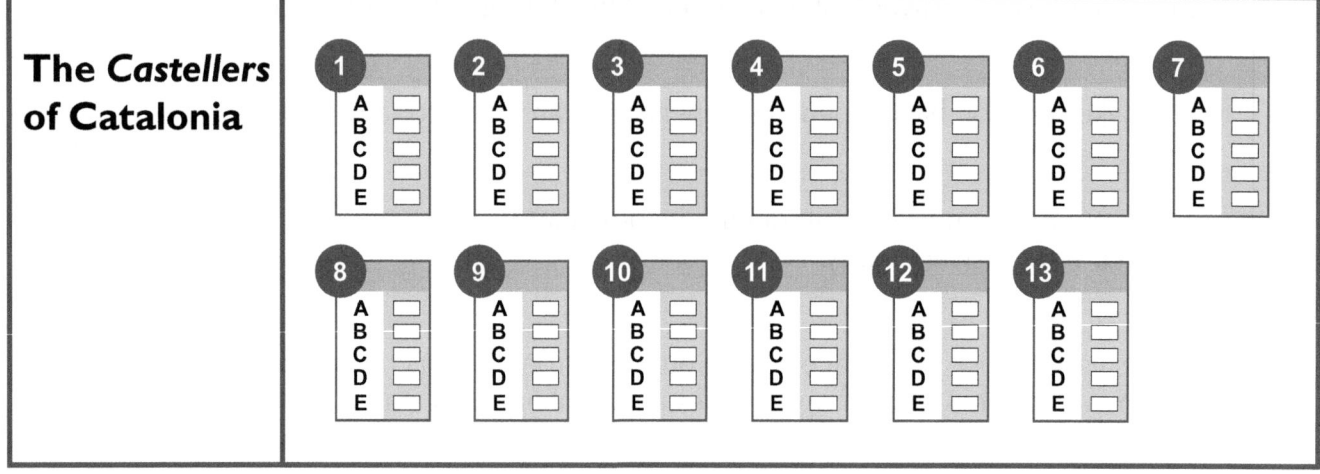

An Unusual Haunting

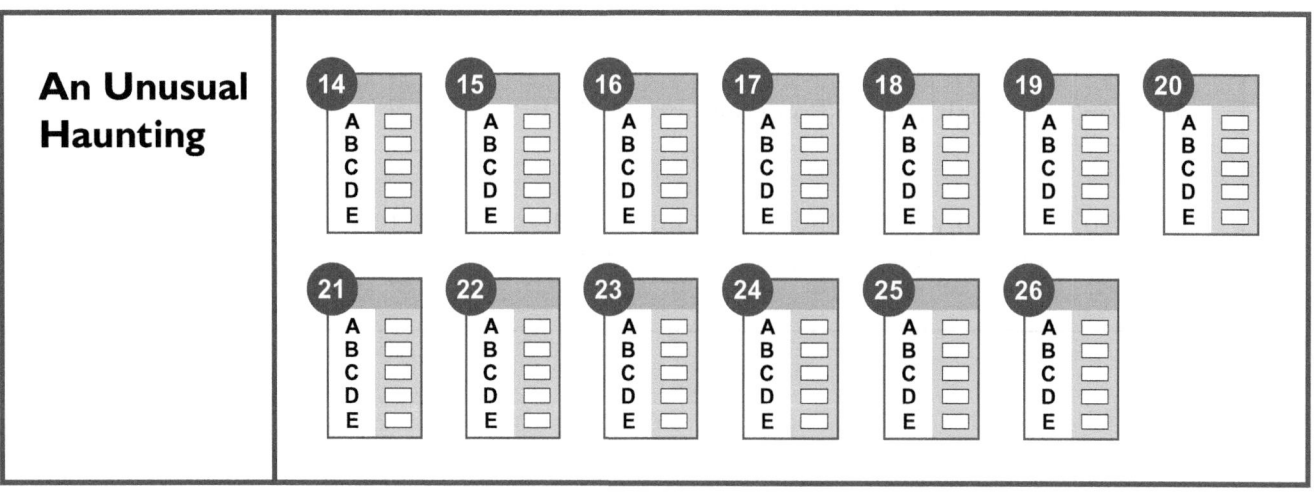

Superb Socks

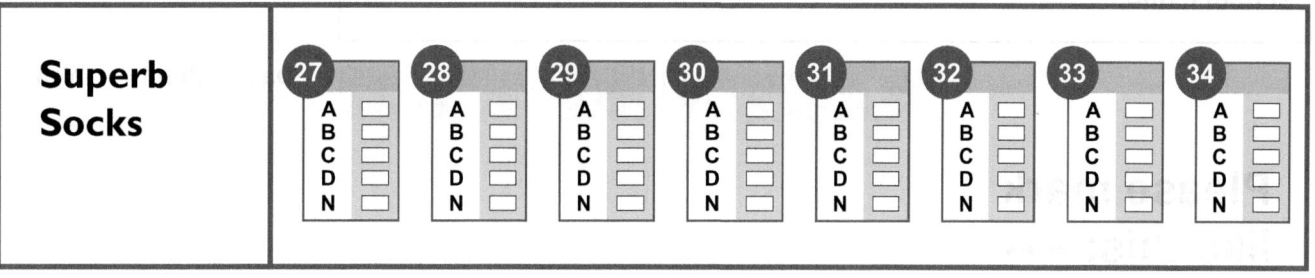

Stuck in the Mud

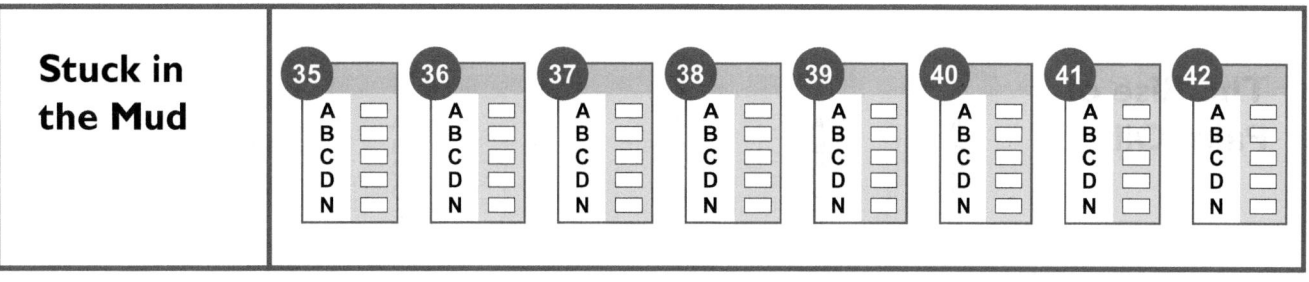

Kanin-hoppning

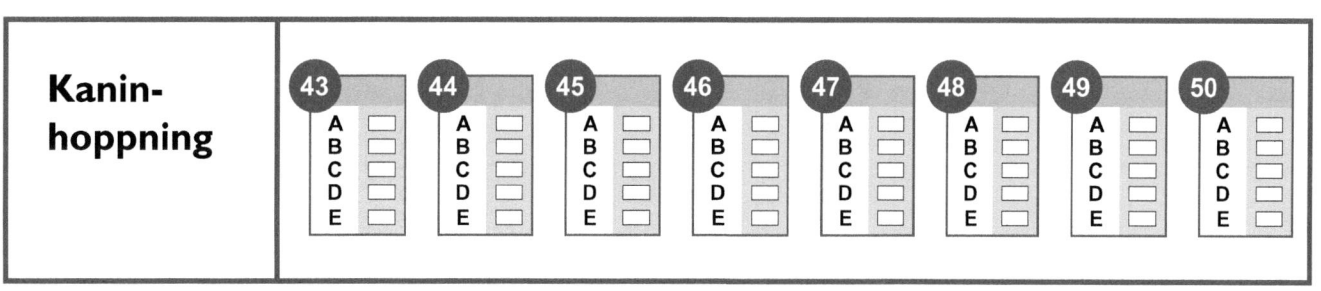

English Practice Paper 6

Pupil's name:

Test date:

School name:

Please mark like this: ▭

Paper 6

Pupil Number

[0]	[0]	[0]	[0]	[0]	[0]
[1]	[1]	[1]	[1]	[1]	[1]
[2]	[2]	[2]	[2]	[2]	[2]
[3]	[3]	[3]	[3]	[3]	[3]
[4]	[4]	[4]	[4]	[4]	[4]
[5]	[5]	[5]	[5]	[5]	[5]
[6]	[6]	[6]	[6]	[6]	[6]
[7]	[7]	[7]	[7]	[7]	[7]
[8]	[8]	[8]	[8]	[8]	[8]
[9]	[9]	[9]	[9]	[9]	[9]

School Number

[0]	[0]	[0]	[0]	[0]	[0]
[1]	[1]	[1]	[1]	[1]	[1]
[2]	[2]	[2]	[2]	[2]	[2]
[3]	[3]	[3]	[3]	[3]	[3]
[4]	[4]	[4]	[4]	[4]	[4]
[5]	[5]	[5]	[5]	[5]	[5]
[6]	[6]	[6]	[6]	[6]	[6]
[7]	[7]	[7]	[7]	[7]	[7]
[8]	[8]	[8]	[8]	[8]	[8]
[9]	[9]	[9]	[9]	[9]	[9]

Date of Birth

Day	Month	Year
[0] [0]	January	2005
[1] [1]	February	2006
[2] [2]	March	2007
[3] [3]	April	2008
[4]	May	2009
[5]	June	2010
[6]	July	2011
[7]	August	2012
[8]	September	2013
[9]	October	2014
	November	2015
	December	2016

The Rise of Palm Oil

1. A B C D E
2. A B C D E
3. A B C D E
4. A B C D E
5. A B C D E
6. A B C D E
7. A B C D E
8. A B C D E
9. A B C D E
10. A B C D E
11. A B C D E
12. A B C D E
13. A B C D E
14. A B C D E
15. A B C D E
16. A B C D E
17. A B C D E
18. A B C D E
19. A B C D E
20. A B C D E
21. A B C D E
22. A B C D E
23. A B C D E
24. A B C D E
25. A B C D E
26. A B C D E

A Worried Wizard

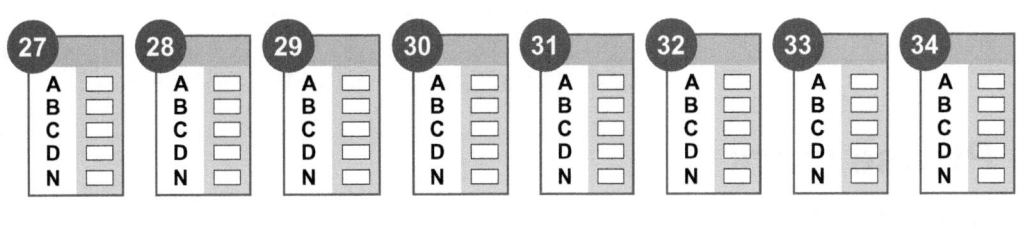

The Grand Opening

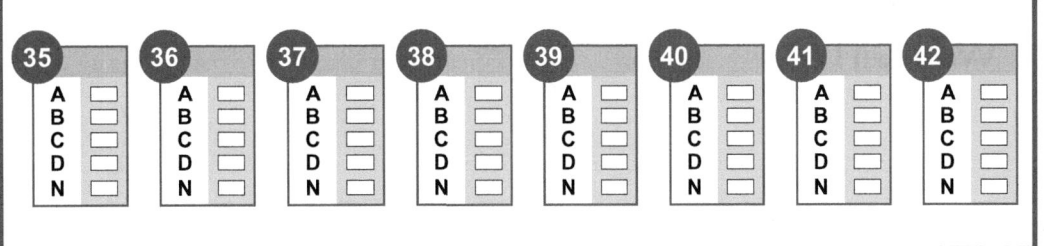

Sun, Sea and Sand

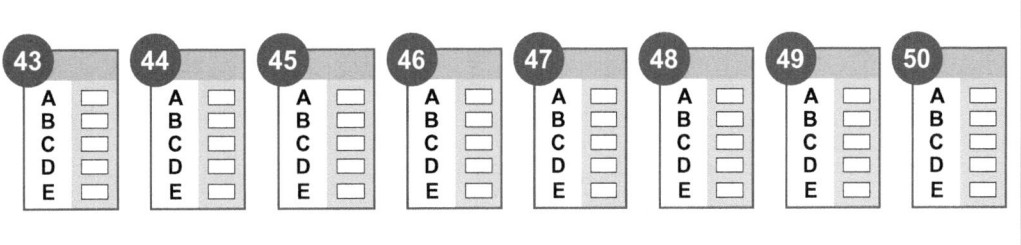

English Practice Paper 7

Pupil's name:

Test date:

School name:

Please mark like this: ⊡

Paper 7

Pupil Number

[0]	[0]	[0]	[0]	[0]	[0]
[1]	[1]	[1]	[1]	[1]	[1]
[2]	[2]	[2]	[2]	[2]	[2]
[3]	[3]	[3]	[3]	[3]	[3]
[4]	[4]	[4]	[4]	[4]	[4]
[5]	[5]	[5]	[5]	[5]	[5]
[6]	[6]	[6]	[6]	[6]	[6]
[7]	[7]	[7]	[7]	[7]	[7]
[8]	[8]	[8]	[8]	[8]	[8]
[9]	[9]	[9]	[9]	[9]	[9]

School Number

[0]	[0]	[0]	[0]	[0]	[0]	[0]
[1]	[1]	[1]	[1]	[1]	[1]	[1]
[2]	[2]	[2]	[2]	[2]	[2]	[2]
[3]	[3]	[3]	[3]	[3]	[3]	[3]
[4]	[4]	[4]	[4]	[4]	[4]	[4]
[5]	[5]	[5]	[5]	[5]	[5]	[5]
[6]	[6]	[6]	[6]	[6]	[6]	[6]
[7]	[7]	[7]	[7]	[7]	[7]	[7]
[8]	[8]	[8]	[8]	[8]	[8]	[8]
[9]	[9]	[9]	[9]	[9]	[9]	[9]

Date of Birth

Day	Month		Year	
[0] [0]	January		2005	
[1] [1]	February		2006	
[2] [2]	March		2007	
[3] [3]	April		2008	
[4]	May		2009	
[5]	June		2010	
[6]	July		2011	
[7]	August		2012	
[8]	September		2013	
[9]	October		2014	
	November		2015	
	December		2016	

Walsall Wolf Girl

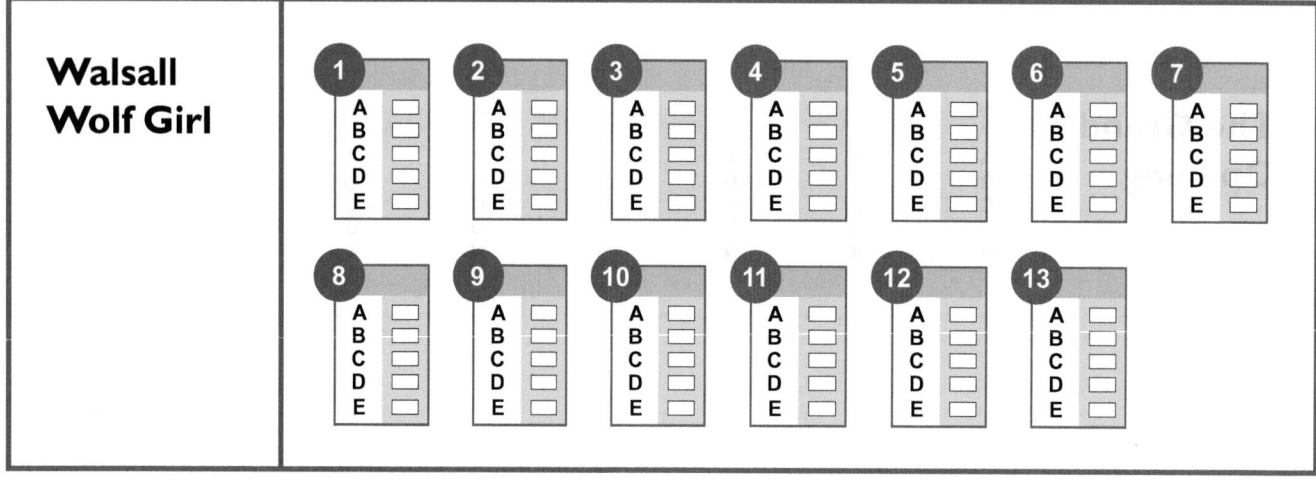

A Human Computer

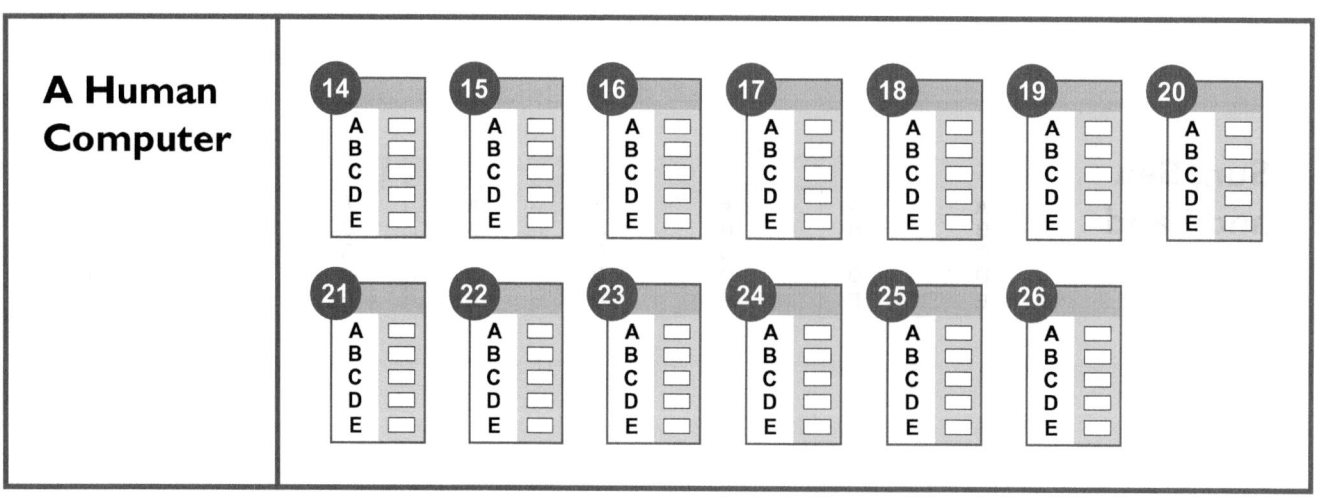

A Crafty Character

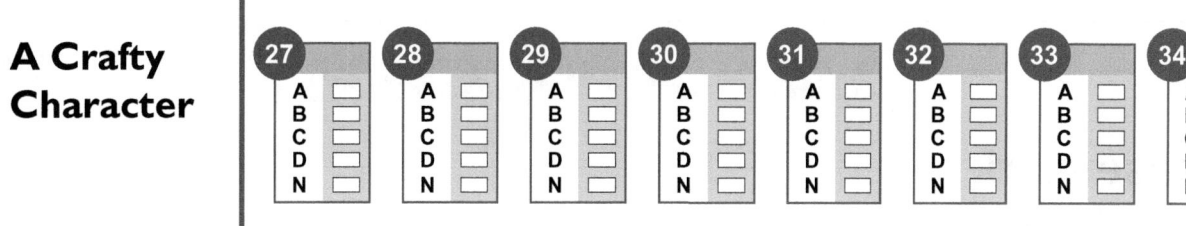

Diving with Sharks

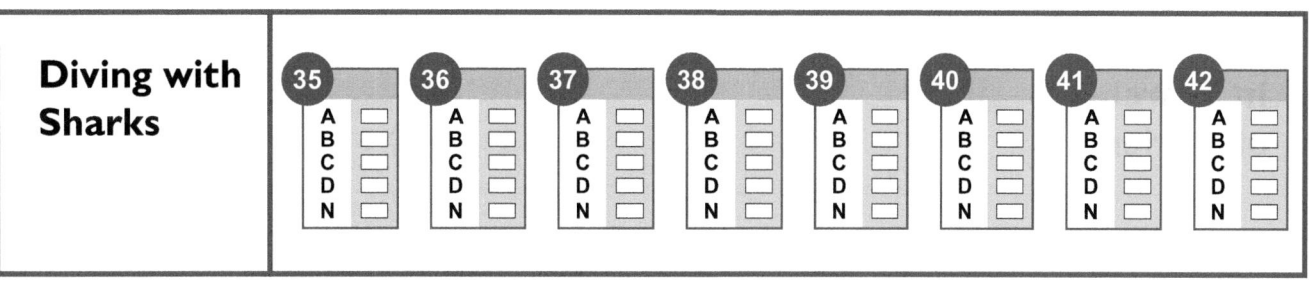

Haircut from Hell

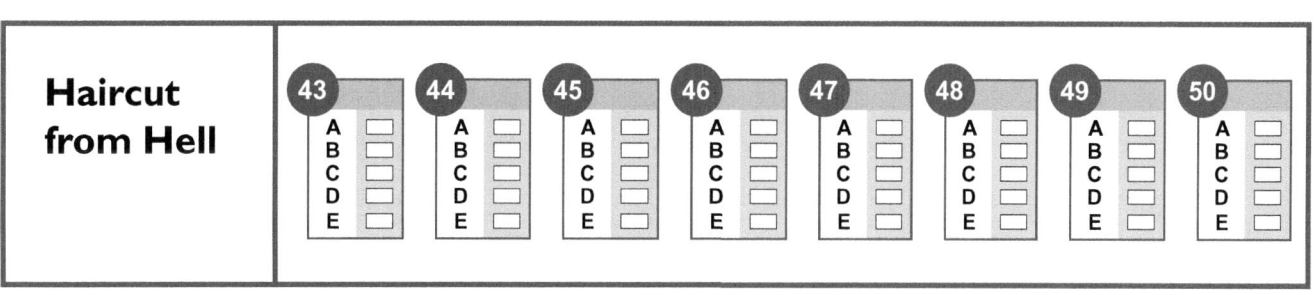

Pupil's name:

School name:

Test date:

Please mark like this: ▭

Paper 8

Pupil Number

| [0] [0] [0] [0] [0] [0] |
| [1] [1] [1] [1] [1] [1] |
| [2] [2] [2] [2] [2] [2] |
| [3] [3] [3] [3] [3] [3] |
| [4] [4] [4] [4] [4] [4] |
| [5] [5] [5] [5] [5] [5] |
| [6] [6] [6] [6] [6] [6] |
| [7] [7] [7] [7] [7] [7] |
| [8] [8] [8] [8] [8] [8] |
| [9] [9] [9] [9] [9] [9] |

School Number

| [0] [0] [0] [0] [0] [0] |
| [1] [1] [1] [1] [1] [1] |
| [2] [2] [2] [2] [2] [2] |
| [3] [3] [3] [3] [3] [3] |
| [4] [4] [4] [4] [4] [4] |
| [5] [5] [5] [5] [5] [5] |
| [6] [6] [6] [6] [6] [6] |
| [7] [7] [7] [7] [7] [7] |
| [8] [8] [8] [8] [8] [8] |
| [9] [9] [9] [9] [9] [9] |

Date of Birth

Day	Month	Year
[0] [0]	January	2005
[1] [1]	February	2006
[2] [2]	March	2007
[3] [3]	April	2008
[4]	May	2009
[5]	June	2010
[6]	July	2011
[7]	August	2012
[8]	September	2013
[9]	October	2014
	November	2015
	December	2016

In Search of a Friend

1 A B C D E
2 A B C D E
3 A B C D E
4 A B C D E
5 A B C D E
6 A B C D E
7 A B C D E
8 A B C D E
9 A B C D E
10 A B C D E
11 A B C D E
12 A B C D E
13 A B C D E
14 A B C D E
15 A B C D E
16 A B C D E
17 A B C D E
18 A B C D E
19 A B C D E
20 A B C D E
21 A B C D E
22 A B C D E
23 A B C D E
24 A B C D E
25 A B C D E
26 A B C D E

Cutlery
Crook
Caught

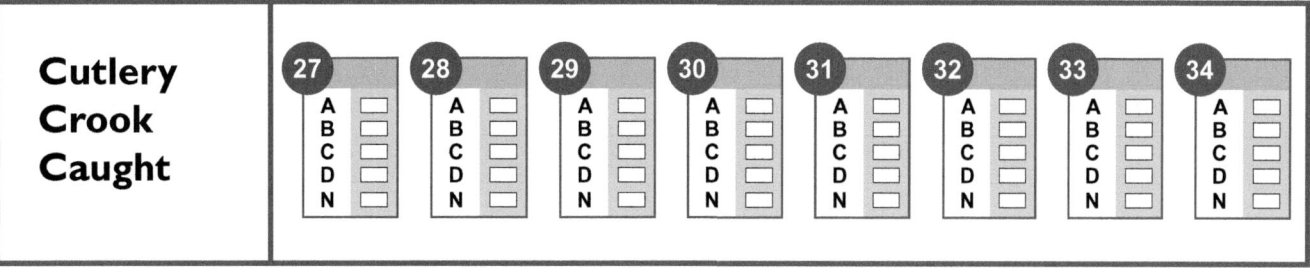

Picture
Perfect

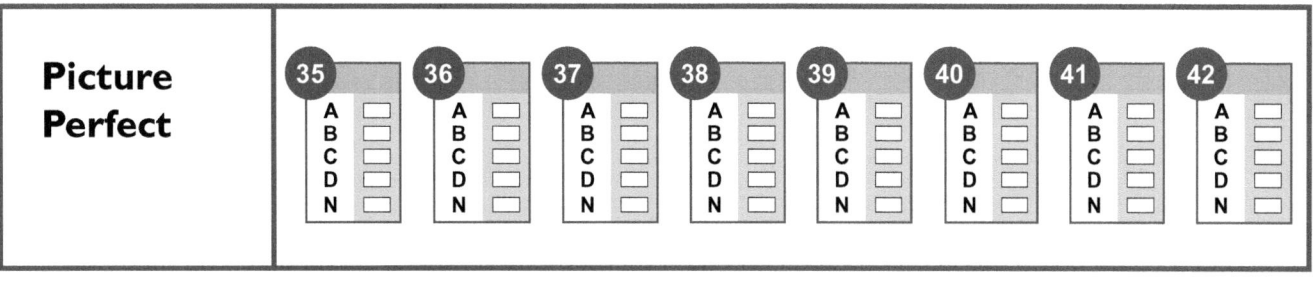

How to
Make a
Pompom

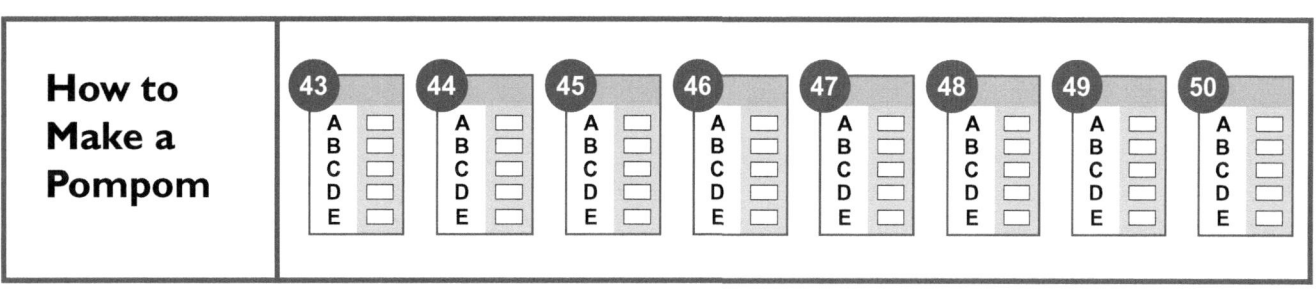

11+ English

For **GL** Assessment

Parents' Guide

Ages 10-11

Pack 2

Published by CGP

Editors:

Siân Butler, Rebecca Greaves, Catherine Heygate and Hannah Roscoe

Many thanks to Sean Walsh for the proofreading.

ISBN: 978 1 78908 697 3

Printed by Elanders Ltd, Newcastle upon Tyne
Clipart from Corel®

What This Pack Contains

What this pack contains

This pack contains **four** 11+ English Practice Papers for the GL test.

The questions in these papers have been written to match the level of difficulty of the real exam. They are designed to test your child's comprehension skills, as well as their spelling, punctuation and grammar.

Each of the practice papers in this pack has an accompanying **multiple-choice answer sheet**, just like the answer sheets used in the real 11+ exams. There are also **full answers** to every question in the separate **answer booklet**.

You can also download and play the **online audio instructions**, which are similar to the instructions that your child will hear on test day. (Depending on the format of the test in your area, the instructions could be played as an audio recording, like the ones we have provided, or they may be read aloud by an exam invigilator.)

You can find the audio downloads at:

cgpbooks.co.uk/11plustestaudio

This set of papers also includes a **free Online Edition**. For details of how to access your Online Edition, just follow the instructions in the box below:

How to access your free Online Edition

This book includes a free Online Edition to read on your PC, Mac or tablet.
You'll just need to go to **cgpbooks.co.uk/extras** and enter this code:

2859 7812 3760 2977

By the way, this code only works for one person. If somebody else has used this book before you, they might have already claimed the Online Edition.

The pages that follow in this Parents' Guide are designed to give some guidance and information on how to best prepare for the 11+ test, as well as how to support your child in performing as well as they can.

- It's important to remember that preparing to take the 11+ can be a stressful time for both parents and pupils. You should do all you can to minimise pressure for the whole family, and try to make the whole process as positive an experience as possible.
- When studying for the 11+, your child will learn plenty of new skills that can have a beneficial impact on their whole education, regardless of whether they pass the 11+ test.
- With the right mindset and preparation, your child will be able to approach the test with confidence, and come out of it feeling positive about their performance.

What is the 11+?

It can be tricky to find reliable information about the 11+ and how to prepare for it. This page covers the basics — what the 11+ test is and how it works.

The 11+ is a selective test

Most secondary schools in the UK are comprehensive — they're non-selective and accept children of all abilities. But in some areas, selective state secondary schools (grammar schools) still exist. These schools select their pupils based on academic ability.

The 11+ test is used to determine if a child is suitable for grammar school. It's also used for entry to some independent schools. Children usually sit the test in the first term of their last year at primary school.

Some schools select pupils based just on the 11+ test results, but others look at other factors, e.g. whether you live close to the school, or if you have other children at the school.

The format of the test varies

The exact format of the 11+ test varies depending on the school or Local Authority (LA) you're applying to, as well as on the provider that sets the test. The main test provider for the 11+ is **GL Assessment**. However, in some cases, the test papers will be written by the school, or by a consortium of schools in that area.

Make sure you know who is responsible for the test in your area, and find out as much information as you can about the format of the test before you start.

Wherever you are, there are four main subjects that can be tested:

> **Verbal Reasoning** — problem-solving and logic using words, letters, numbers, etc.
> **Non-Verbal Reasoning** — problem-solving and logic using pictures and symbols.
> **Maths** — often at the same level as the SATs, but it may be more challenging.
> **English** — reading comprehension, grammar and sometimes a writing task.

Tests set by GL Assessment can include any combination of these four subjects (you won't necessarily have to do all four). Traditionally, there would be a different test paper for each subject — however, some GL exams now include mixed papers, with two papers that each cover more than one subject. Check the format of the test in your region well in advance of test day.

The tests are usually either **multiple choice** (MC) or **standard answer** (SA) format.

> **Multiple choice** — there's a separate answer sheet. There's usually a choice of five options for each answer, and the answers may be computer-marked.
> **Standard answer** — there are spaces on the question paper for the pupil to write their own answers. There will usually not be any answer options given for the pupil to choose from.

Using the Practice Papers

This advice will help you to get the most out of this set of practice papers. You may wish to administer the practice papers in exam conditions to help your child become familiar with the format of the test.

These practice papers are in multiple-choice format

There is advice on filling in the multiple-choice answer sheets on page 3 of the answer sheet booklet. Read through this advice with your child before you begin. Make sure that they understand what they need to do before they begin a paper, and that they are filling in the answer sheet which matches the paper they are attempting.

How to set the practice papers

- Do the practice papers at a time when your child usually works well. This might be a weekday after school, or at the weekend. This will help them work to the best of their abilities.

- As you get closer to the actual test, it is a good idea to sit some practice papers at the same time of day as the real thing — that way, your child will be used to the routine and there shouldn't be any surprises.

- Your child should attempt the practice paper at a clear table in a quiet area, free from distractions and interruptions.

- They'll need a sharp pencil, an eraser and a pencil sharpener.

- You can play the online audio to mimic real exam conditions. The audio runs through the instructions found on the front of the practice paper, and will give your child information about timings.

- If you're not using the online audio instructions, read out the instructions on the front of the practice paper before your child begins. Make sure that they understand what they have to do. Position your child so they can see a watch or clock so that they can keep track of the time they have left.

- Time the test strictly. If they haven't finished the paper in the time allowed, you could draw a line under the last question they answered within the time limit so you know to give marks up to that point. You can then time them to see how long it takes them to finish the paper. This will allow you to monitor the speed your child is working at.

- Encourage them to read over their answers if they finish within the time limit, but don't give them extra time to do this.

- Mark their test using the answers in the separate answer booklet.

Marking the practice papers

You should give one mark for each correct answer your child gave within the time limit, then work out the total score. It's really important to go through any wrong answers with your child — use the explanations in the answer book to show them how to find the right answer.

The pass mark will vary from school to school and year to year. It's common practice for your child's 'raw score' (i.e. the actual number of questions they answered correctly) to be converted into a 'standardised score'. This helps to make the results fairer by taking your child's age into account, as well as bringing scores for different papers in line with each other. As such, there is no number of correct answers that will guarantee a pass, but for these practice papers, we suggest that your child aims for a score of 85% or more.

Your child's score might help you pinpoint specific skills that they need to practise. For example, if your child scored 60%, got nearly all the questions right, but didn't finish the test, they need to work faster. We have given some advice to help you increase your child's speed on p.6.

If they scored 60%, got to the end, but got 40% of the questions wrong, they need to brush up on their accuracy. You can follow this up with some more practice in the areas they struggled with, then set another practice test.

Improving Your Child's Score

For your child to do well in their 11+, they'll need to work quickly and avoid making mistakes. Here's some advice to help improve your child's score and test technique.

Start by working on accuracy...

When your child is just starting out, it's a good idea to focus on their accuracy and understanding, rather than speed. You can work on their speed when they're a bit more confident.

Once your child has finished a paper and you've marked it, you should go over the questions they got wrong, so they know how they should have answered them. You could even come back to these trickier questions at a later date to make sure they can still get them right.

...then work on speed

In the real 11+ test, children are deliberately put under time pressure. This helps schools distinguish between good candidates and the best ones. The faster your child is, the more questions they'll answer. Once your child can accurately answer 11+ questions, use these tips to help them improve their speed:

- Find out the timings of the real test — how long your child will have, and how many questions they'll have to answer. When they're practising, give them slightly less time than this to do the same number of questions.
- Encourage your child only to check their answers if they have time at the end of the test.
- You could introduce games to get them working faster — try using a stopwatch to time a set of questions, and get your child to ring a bell or shout when they've finished them.
- For comprehension questions, it's important that your child can read the text quickly. Encourage them to read the text first, then look at the questions — remind them that they can look back at the text as many times as they like when answering the questions.

In the run-up to the test, start working on test technique

Your child will score better on the 11+ if they improve their test technique. Good test technique is also important for their SATs, and other exams later in their education. When they start working through assessment papers, remind them to do the following things:

- Read the front of the paper and enter the correct information on it.
- Skip any questions that are really difficult, or which are taking a long time — they can come back to them if there's time at the end.
- If they can't do a question and they're running out of time, make a sensible guess. For multiple-choice questions, they may be able to rule out one or two options that definitely aren't correct, which gives a better chance of guessing which of the remaining ones is right.

If your child's test is in multiple-choice format, there are some other specific techniques to practise:

- Marking the correct box neatly and quickly using a horizontal line.
- Making sure they mark the answer in the correct box, especially if they skip a question.
- If they don't finish the paper, filling in the rest of the answers randomly.

When your child does a practice paper, they should work in silence and without help. Try to make their experience as close to the real test as possible.

What to Expect on Test Day

The test day and the time before you get the results can be just as stressful for you as for your child. Here are some tips about how to reduce this stress, and how to cope with the waiting period.

Facing the test

Make sure you and your child are fully prepared for the day of the test. You need to know:

- Where the test is and how you're going to get there (parking may be difficult).
- What time the test starts and what time you need to arrive by.
- What they'll need to take (pencils, etc.) or whether everything is provided for them.

Make sure your child is as relaxed as possible the night before the test, and that they get a good night's sleep. A healthy evening meal and breakfast before the test will also help put your child in the right frame of mind to tackle the test. It's also a good idea to talk them through the arrangements for the day so they know what will happen.

After the test, plan an outing or a treat which will take your child's (and your) mind off the test. Even if your child is still preparing for other 11+ tests, they'll need a break.

- There's usually a retest day for children who are ill on the day of the test. Check with the school in advance, and let the test centre know as soon as possible if you can't make it to the test.
- If you think there are circumstances that have affected your child's performance in the test, gather evidence of this as soon as possible (e.g. a doctor's note or school marks that have dipped). Once you've got the results it'll be too late.

After the 11+

Make a plan for the time between the last of your child's tests and the day you get their results — this wait can be very stressful.

If you're going to reward your child for their hard work preparing for the 11+, you might want to do it now. If they're rewarded for their effort and hard work, they'll realise that they've achieved something, even if their results aren't what they hoped for.

Remind your child that you are proud of them no matter what the outcome, and try not to build up results day as too big a deal. If your child is unsuccessful, then it's not the end of the world. If your child does gain a grammar school place, then make sure they're aware that some of their classmates might not have done, and may need a friend to help make them feel better.

If you feel there is good reason, then this is also a good time to research the appeals process for the schools you've applied to. Some parents choose to appeal the admission decision if their child isn't offered a place.

Make sure you have an alternative plan

For some grammar schools, there can be several applicants for each available place. Even if your child scores highly on the test, it may still not be enough to gain a place at the school. You should put at least one non-selective school on your secondary school application form — it's a good idea to have visited these schools, so your child knows what to expect if they aren't offered a grammar school place.

It's important that your child doesn't feel like a failure if they don't get into a grammar school — there are many excellent comprehensive schools where your child can be happy and successful. Remember that school is what you make it, and a positive response to not gaining a grammar school place is key to this.